PRAYER: AN INVITATION FROM GOD

Charles Nieman

**All Scripture quotations
from the *King James Version*
of the Bible unless otherwise stated**

ISBN 0-914307-03-7

**Printed in the United States of America
Copyright © 1983 WORD OF FAITH PUBLISHING
PO Box 819000, Dallas, Texas 75381
All Rights Reserved**

Cover photo by John W. Tozier-WORD OF FAITH

TABLE OF CONTENTS

I.	Prayer Fundamentals	1
II.	Steps to Answered Prayer	19
III.	Building a Prayer Habit	25
IV.	The Enemies of Prayer	35
V.	Kinds of Prayer	41
VI.	Intercessory Prayer	57
VII.	Interceding Against the Powers of Darkness	73
VIII.	Interceding for the Saints	89
IX.	Interceding for the Nation	101
X.	The Prayer of Binding and Loosing	111
XI.	The Prayer of Agreement	115
XII.	The Prayer of Dedication	119
XIII.	Prayer of Committal	123
XIV.	United Prayer	131
XV.	Praying for Your Food	135
XVI.	A Check List for Effective Prayers	139

DEDICATION

This book is dedicated to my wife, Rochelle. She has always believed in me and stood with me, and is my best friend.

Also, to my children, Shannon and Jared, who always understood when I could not play with them as I was writing this book.

INTRODUCTION

Prayer. There is no other subject so closely associated with Christianity. History tells us of the great things that have happened as a result of prayer. God needs each of us to take our place in prayer. The purpose of this book is to encourage you to develop a prayer life that revolves around God's Word, that is effective and exciting! Prayer is God's invitation to you, for you to come and fellowship with Him.

I pray that the things you learn in this book will inform you, inspire you, and increase your knowledge of how valuable you are in God's plans.

CHAPTER I
PRAYER FUNDAMENTALS

Luke 18:1, *"And he spake a parable unto them to this end, that men ought to pray, and not to faint."* In another translation it says that men ought to always pray and not cave in, not give up, not wither. Another translation says that men ought to pray all the time and not turn out badly.

If there is anything in the Bible that is associated with Christianity it is prayer. When you think of Christians you think of prayer. You think of a dear old sister sitting in a room down on her knees praying, or you think of Jesus in the garden of Gethsemane praying. Prayer and Christianity are synonymous terms. We associate them together. When you think of prayer you think of Christians, when you think of Christians you think of prayer. This is a good analogy that we have developed between Christians and prayer because prayer is a vital part of Christianity. Now, the amazing thing is that many Christian people know just enough about prayer to get them into a lot of trouble. Christians realize that prayer is something we are supposed to do. Prayer is something that has been made available to us, but we have stuffed prayer full of religion. As a result, our praying has become of no effect. Jesus said that your religious traditions will make the Word of God of no effect. Religion robs the Word of its power.

Now, in respect to all that, I am going to make some statements to you concerning prayer. E.W. Kenyon said some of the greatest things concerning prayer that I have ever heard. Listen to these statements. Dr. Kenyon said, prayer is our need crying out to God. Prayer is the voice of faith to the Father. He continues by saying that prayer is born of a sense of need and the assurance that the need will be met. That is a revolutionary statement when it comes to prayer in most Christian's minds. Most of us think that prayer is nothing more than telling God about our problems and our needs. "God, I need this, God I want that, God, you have got to do something about this. Oh God, please do that. Oh God, please change this. Oh God, do this. Oh God, do that. Thank you very much. Amen. Goodbye, see you later."

Let us see what the Word says about our need. Matthew 6:32, Jesus speaking, *"For after all these things do the Gentiles seek: (physical needs) for your heavenly Father knoweth that you have need of all these things."* Now, brothers and sisters, we need to become very, very established in this fact. God knows what you have need of even before you ask Him. Doesn't He? When you and I go to Him and say, "Father, I need a hundred dollars," that is not when He found out we needed a hundred dollars. The fact of the matter is, if we had been listening to God, He would have revealed to us long before we had the need, what to do concerning the need, and the need would never have arisen. I am not saying that to put us down. All of us come to points in our lives where we have need of things and God has made provision for those needs. However, the thing I want you to see and understand is God did not design prayer just for us to tell Him our problems. God already knows our problems. He already knows what is wrong. He already knows what we have need of. Family, He knows more about it than we do.

We have developed another kind of mentality concerning prayer. We teach that God has developed prayer because He wants us to tell Him everything we need just because He likes to hear it. He likes for you to tell Him, you see, because that proves to you

His superiority, His greatness and your weakness. I do not agree with that type of thinking. Are you convinced that God is greater than you? I think that is a foregone conclusion in the Body of Christ —that God is superior to us. I am not having any problems with that. Are you having any problems with that? I am not having any problems with thinking that I am in God's league. What then is the purpose for prayer? Why are we supposed to pray? There is more to prayer than just telling God the problem. A lot of what we call prayer is really no more than bellyaching, griping and complaining. That is all it is. For some people prayer is no more than telling God everything that is wrong.

Now, brothers and sisters, that is not what prayer was designed to do. God knows what is wrong. Remember what E.W. Kenyon said? Now, listen to this statement. It will revolutionize your thinking. What I want to do is set your minds on the right track. PRAYER IS NOT JUST TELLING GOD THE PROBLEM. PRAYER IS DOING SOMETHING ABOUT THE PROBLEM. Dr. Kenyon said prayer is our voice of faith. Of what? Of faith. Faith makes everything work in the kingdom of God. Apart from faith you are not going to receive. I do not care how badly we need it. I do not care how badly we want something. I do not care how much we deserve it. I do not care how sweet we are or how unjustly we are being treated. We can go to God all day long and say, "God, what they are doing to me is not right. It is not right that I am in this position." Well you are right, it is not fair. But just see if that changes anything. Just see if your standing there and telling God, "It is not right, it is not right, it is not right," is going to do anything. It will not change anything.

So then, what is prayer? He said it is the **voice of**

faith. It is the voice of faith to our Father. It is us talking to Him concerning our need, with the assurance that the need will be met. That is the barb on the end of the hook concerning prayer. Listen, we have assurance when we pray because we know through prayer we can make something happen concerning the thing we prayed about. Now, if you do not have that confidence when you pray you are wasting your time. Why? Because all you are doing is merely telling God the problem when He already knows the problem. God is well aware of the situation.

I want to share with you some more statements by E.W. Kenyon. Brother Kenyon had great insight into prayer. He said prayer is facing God with needs and His promise to meet those needs. Prayer is facing God with man's needs and His promise to meet those needs.

When I read this next statement my entire concept of prayer was revolutionized. I used to think that prayer was me arm wrestling with God. Have you ever thought like this? "Well, dear me, it is time to pray. I am going to go in there and pray. I better fortify myself. I better get ready for the long siege on the throne of God." I knew a man one time who had a situation in his life and he did not know what to do about it. So, he set out to find out what to do about it. He told his wife that he was going into another part of his house and was going to stay in prayer until God answered him concerning this problem. He gathered up food and about six or seven quarts of soft drinks, hauled all this stuff into this other part of his house and went into this room. He was determined to stay and pray until God answered him. He was in there about twenty minutes surrounded with sandwiches and quarts of soft drink. Now, I am saying all that to you because this man's attitude in prayer was similar to many of our attitudes in prayer. He figured he was going to have to go in there and bang on the throne until God finally answered.

Brothers and sisters, getting the Lord's attention is not our problem. I can tell you how to get God's attention. The way to get God's attention is to say "Father, in the name of Jesus." You have His attention — He is listening to you. When you speak that name out of your lips, you have the ear of God. Now, that sounds too simple doesn't it? That is the whole problem with many people. It is too simple, and they want to complicate it. "Well now, brother, I'm not too sure about that. I believe in fasting and prayer." Great, so do I. But family, it is not fasting that gets God's attention. God can fast a lot longer than you. So, do not think that your great record of missing lunch is going to impress God, especially when the whole time you miss lunch you are sitting around saying, "Oh dear God, I am so hungry." And your stomach is growling, your head is hurting, you are weak, slouching around and getting grouchy and upset at everybody. I tell you the Lord would rather you didn't fast if that is how you are going to act. I have seen some people go on fasts and the whole world pays. All the angels are glad when they finally go off that fast. Now, the Bible talks about fasting and prayer, but we will discuss that later.

You see, prayer is not designed for you to grab hold of the arm of god and twist it until He says, "Alright, alright you can have it, you can have it." That is not the purpose for prayer. The Bible does not say for you to go wrestle with God. "Well, Charles I am going to be like Jacob." Well, go ahead. Go out there and wrestle with God. Maybe you will get your hip knocked out of joint like he did. No, you see we have got to get over those ideas. That is not what prayer is designed to do.

Prayer is God's invitation to us to fellowship with Him. God has sent an invitation to us to come and fellowship with him and that invitation is called prayer. Isn't that beautiful? That will revolutionize your thinking concerning prayer.

Now, there are times when you will come before God, stand in the gap in intercessory prayer, cry out to God, wrestle with demonic powers, grab hold of the Word of God, and hold on until you can bring God and this person whom you are praying for into contact with one another. There have been times when I have gotten down on the floor and have cried out to God and said, "No, they won't die, they won't die, they won't die," and I have stayed there until I knew in my heart I had won. Now, there are times for that and we will get into that later in this book. But that is not all the time. The attitude in prayer is not one of, "Well dear God, here we go. Send the kids over to the grandparents. We have got to pray. We may be at this for nine days." If that is your attitude and image, that is exactly how long it is going to take. Prayer is God's invitation to you to come and fellowship with Him.

THE INTEGRAL PART OF PRAYER

Your fellowship with God and His fellowship with you revolve around one central point. Do you know what it is? What is the one thing that you and God have in common — that both of you can agree upon? It is His Word! God is doing things that you and I do not know about and He is involved in areas that we do not have any knowledge of. But there is a central point that we can agree upon; to where His thoughts and our thoughts can be one and that is through His Word. **HIS WORD IS OUR CENTRAL AGREEMENT POINT.** That is the point of fellowship that we have. God's Word is the central, integral, most critical part of prayer.

UNANSWERED PRAYER

Let's read James 4:1-8, *"From whence come wars and fighting among you? come they not hence, even of your lusts that war in your member? Ye lust, and have not: ye kill, and desire to have and cannot obtain: ye fight and war, yet ye have not, because ye ask not. Ye ask, and receive not, because ye ask amiss, that ye may consume it upon your lusts. Ye adulterers and adulteresses, know ye not that the friendship of the world is enmity with God? whosoever therefore will be a friend of the world is the enemy of God.* That is pretty straight — isn't it? *Do ye think that the scriptures saith in vain, The spirit that dwelleth in us lusteth to envy? But he giveth more grace. Wherefore he saith, God resisteth the proud, but giveth grace unto the humble. Submit yourselves therefore to God. Resist the devil, and he will flee from you. Draw nigh to God, and he will draw nigh to you ..."* Notice verses 3-4. He said that you ask and receive not because you ask amiss that you may consume it upon your lusts. Now, there has been a lot of discussion among Christian people concerning this verse of scripture and it bears a lot of discussion, especially in the light of statements Jesus made concerning prayer.

He said in Mark 11:24 that whatsoever things you desire, when you pray, believe that you receive them and you shall have them. In the Gospel of Matthew the twenty-first chapter He said that what things soever you ask in prayer believing you shall receive. But, in the book of James he said that you ask and receive not because you ask amiss. Now, it appears that a contradiction is seen in these verses. Jesus said whatever you ask for you will receive. James said whatever you ask for you might not get. The answer to the whole thing is found in I John chapter 5. You might say "Charles, how come the answer is in I John — why wasn't the answer in the other scriptures?" From the standpoint of God it is all in the same book. It does not make any difference to Him if John's name is on it or Matthew's name is on it or Peter's name is on it, because He is the one who wrote it. We are the ones who put in the chapter titles and the chapter divisions and the book titles and all — not God.

I John 5:14-15, *"And this is the confidence that we have in him, that, if we ask any thing according to his will, he heareth us: And if we know that he hears us, whatsoever we ask, we know that we have the petitions that we desired of him."* Now that's pretty good — isn't it? It says we have this confidence, that if we ask anything of the Lord according to His will, He hears us.

"I'm not sure if God heard me when I prayed." Did you pray according to His will? "Well, I don't know." What do you mean you don't know? "I mean nobody knows what the will of God is." Oh, yes we do! His will and His Word are exactly the same.

"But Charles, I never found a scripture that says the Lord wants me to have a new car." You haven't? You haven't found that verse of scripture? I found that verse of scripture. "What kind of translation does that boy have?" Same one you have, I just read mine. "There's no scripture that says anything about new cars." Sure there is. It is called Phillippians 4:19, *"But my God shall supply all your need according to his riches in glory by Christ Jesus."* I also found Mark 11:24, *"...what things soever ye desire, when ye pray, believe ye receive them, and ye shall have them"* "Yes, but He is not talking about cars." Alright, go ahead — go figure out how to get one on your own. I'm going to pray and believe God. It works too!

Now, many Christians have read that verse of scripture and because we have been so fruitless in prayer, we have come up with little Christian cliches to answer our fruitlessness. 'Father, we're asking you in the name of Jesus to do such and such if it be Thy will. Amen."

Now, let me make some statements here to you concerning prayer. Do not get religious with God. A lot of people think when they pray they have to pray in King James English. God knows that is not the way you talk all day long. So why are you trying to fool Him and come in and start talking "thees" and "thous"? In addition, you do not know how to talk King James English right anyway — you are going to do it all wrong. Most people do not talk everyday regular English right, least yet King James English. So why are you trying to fool God? "Isn't that how God talks"? No, that is how King James talked. That is not how God talks. Now, if that is the only way that you can hear God, then that is the only way God will talk to you. Some people would not believe the Lord spoke to them if He spoke in everyday English. I'm serious. Have you heard people try to pray in Old English? They make up words. "If thou wouldst Lordst." They think by doing that the Lord will say, "Listen to that. Oh, now meet that boy's needs." What does God care? It does not matter to Him. It does not matter to the Lord at all. They want to put that little tag on, "If it be thy will. Father, in the name of Jesus, I'd like for you to give me a hundred dollars by Friday, if it be thy will." If what you prayed up until that point was not the will of

God, He did not hear it anyway and your throwing that little tag on there is not going to get Him to hear it. Does that make sense to you? Remember the scripture that we just read, *"And this is the confidence that we have in Him, that, if we ask anything according to his will, he hears us: And if we know that he hears us, whatsoever we ask, we know that we have the petitions we desired of him."*

KEY TO ANSWERED PRAYER

So, the key to answered prayer is what? Get God to hear you. How do you get God to hear you? You must pray according to His will. What is His will? HIS WILL IS HIS WORD! Now, God and His Word and God and His will are inseparable. God does not will one thing and say another. God means what He says and says what He means! God does not play word games with us. Do you know why? Because He and His Word are inseparable. In fact, He is so much like His Word that in John the first chapter He said that in the beginning the Word was God. The Word was God. God and His Word are the same. Now the Word has got to be the integral, central part of prayer. Your prayers must revolve around the Word.

Eventually, I will show you and you will learn how to pray God's Word. "Well, what good is that?" It guarantees you that God will hear you. It guarantees that God will hear you and when God hears you, you receive. Now, if there is anything I like, I like to get answers to prayer. Don't you?

I want to show you something else. Turn to John 15:1 and I will show you that God likes for you to get answers in prayer. E.W. Kenyon said that prayer is not a slavish duty but a privilege. John 15:1-3, Jesus speaking, *"I am the true vine, and my Father is the husbandman. Every branch in me that beareth not fruit he taketh away: and every branch that beareth fruit, he purgeth it, that it may bring forth more fruit. Now ye are clean through the word which I have spoken unto you."* The word "purge" in verse 2 and the word "clean" in verse 3 are the same words in the original text. *"Now ye are clean* (or you are purged) *through the word which I have spoken unto you."*

Remember that God does not — does not— does not purge the church with sickness and disease, tests and trials, hard times or getting fired from your job. That is not how God purges the Church. What does God use to purge the church? The Word. What does He use? The Word.

Verses 4-6, *"Abide in me, and I in you. As the branch cannot bear fruit of itself, except it abide in the vine; no more can ye, except ye abide in me. I am the vine, you are the branches: He that abideth in me, and I in him, the same bringeth forth much fruit: for without me ye can do nothing. If a man abide not in me, he is cast forth as a branch, and is withered; and men gather them, and cast them into the fire and they are burned."* Look again at verses 7 and 8, *"If ye abide in me, and my words abide in you, ye shall ask what ye will, and it* (it what? — it that you asked) *shall be done unto you. Herein is my Father glorified that ye bear much fruit ..."*

When does God receive glory? When we bear fruit. How do we bear fruit? By abiding in Christ and His Word abiding in you. You doing what? Asking what you will. It is done how? According to what you will — herein is God glorified. When is God glorified? When you get answered prayer. That brings God glory. Isn't that good? Do you want to glorify God? Well, praise God, start praying. Start getting answers to your prayers. That is how God receives glory. No, God does not receive glory with you being sick. "Well, God will get glory out of me staying here at home in the bed today." No, God is not going to get glory out of that.

In the ministry of Jesus, He received glory everytime somebody got healed or delivered. At the gate Beautiful (Acts 3:6-8) when Peter and John walked up to the lame man there and Peter said, *"...Silver and gold have I none; but such as I have give I thee: In the name of Jesus Christ of Nazareth rise up and walk. And he took him by the right hand, and lifted him up: and immediately his feet and ankle bones received strength. And he leaping up stood, and walked, and entered with them into the temple, walking, and leaping, and praising God."* When did God receive glory? When the man got healed. That is when God received glory.

God receives glory when His power is made evident in the earth. God's power revolves around His Word. If you find the power of God you find the Word of God there too. And if you find the Word you will find the power because you cannot separate them.

Luke 4:32 says, *"And they were astonished at his doctrine: for his word was with power."* They said His Word was with power. They did not say His Word had power. They said His Word was with power. His Word was with power. If you come into a building and your husband or wife is with you, people say you are with each other. His Word is how? With power.

Every time I read that I get an image of God's Word and power walking around with their arms hooked with each other. Wherever one of them goes, the other one goes. They cannot be separated. His Word is with power. You find the Word and you find power.

Family, you must find out what the Word says because that is where the power is — in the Word. You cannot get ahold of the power of God apart from His Word. I do not care how badly you need it.

"I tell you, Charles, if something does not happen today we're going under." Then you better find out what the Word says because that is where the power is. "Well, I don't have the time to read or study or confess the Bible." I'm sorry that is the case, because for all practical purposes you are going to fail.

Remember, God's invitation to you is to come and fellowship with Him. Think about that today. Write that down on a little card and put it right next to your bed. When you get up in the morning pick it up and just read it a couple of times and put that thought into your mind. Then during the day run it over in your mind. I guarantee you that you will spend time with your heavenly Father today that you did not know you could spend.

Now, many of us have had a great amount of knowledge given to us in the area of prayer. Most people think they are very knowledgeable in the area of prayer and I'm not saying that they aren't. But, I am saying that prayer is vital in Christianity and for that reason prayer demands our study and attention to the fine details. Oftentimes, when people know nothing about a subject, it is easier to teach them on that subject than it is to teach them on a subject that they have some knowledge of. Why? Because oftentimes, when people have knowledge of a subject they are convinced that they have all knowledge. As a result, it is very hard to teach them.

THE PEARL

In Matthew the seventh chapter, Jesus reveals some outstanding truths concerning life in general, and prayer specifically. Jesus speaking beginning in verse 1, *"Judge not, that ye be not judged. For with what judgment ye judge, ye shall be judged: and with what measure ye mete, it shall be measured to you again. And why beholdest thou the mote that is in thy brother's eye, but considerest not the beam that is in thine own eye?"* That is very strong isn't it? *"Or how wilt thou say to thy brother, Let me pull out the mote out of thine eye; and, behold, a beam is in thine own eye?"* Now, the word "mote" literally means a splinter. He is telling us that before we attempt to remove the splinter out of someone else's eye we need to remove the beam out of our own eye. Before you try to clean up someone else's house, clean your own first.

He continues saying, *"Thou hypocrite, first cast out the beam out of thine own eye; and then shalt thou see clearly to cast out the mote out of thy brother's eye. Give not that which is holy unto the dogs, neither cast ye your pearls before swine, lest they trample them under their feet, and turn again and rend you."* Now, verse six is an interesting verse. A lot of people read it and think that Jesus is saying number one, you should not have anything to do with dogs and number two, do not take your pearls that your mother left you and throw them down before the pigs. I do not think that is what Jesus is talking about here, do you? What He is saying to us is to be careful and to watch ourselves so that we do not take things that are valuable — the things of God, and misuse them.

Later in this chapter, Jesus teaches on the pearl of great price. That pearl is the kingdom of God. He said all things that can be desired cannot be compared to this pearl of great price. Now, He says do not take the pearls or the things of God's Word that are valuable to you and cast them before the swine.

14

The swine that He is making reference to here are things that are unclean. In other words do not put the valuable things of God's Word in a position where people can trample them underfoot.

Yes, we need to witness and we need to share our faith in the Lord Jesus Christ, because that is how the Gospel is preached. People find out about the things of God by one-on-one testimony. The greatest evangelistic tool in the earth today is one-on-one testimony.

However, in the course of your witnessing and your talking to people, realize that there are certain things in your life that are very valuable to you. Do not take those pearls and cast them out in front of people who do not appreciate them, who don't want anything to do with them. Of course, it is going to happen to a certain degree accidentally. But there are always some people who you need to be careful what you tell them about in respect to God's promises, because they will take the things that you share and throw them down and stomp all over them. They will not have anything to do with them.

There are certain people I know that I cannot talk to about healing because they attack it and they throw it down and they ridicule it and they make fun of it. I am not going to talk to them about it. Some may say, "Are you afraid to talk to them, Charles, because they might talk you out of believing in healing?" No. But I am not going to cast my pearls before the swine. I am not going to take things that are valuable to me and throw them before the swine. Even in the natural realm you do not take things that are valuable and give them to just anybody to mess around with because not everybody appreciates them.

Now, the same thing is true from a spiritual standpoint. A lot of the things that are valuable to you, at times you need to keep them to yourself, because some people — no, not everybody — but some people will trample them under foot. Do you know who that is going to hurt? It is going to hurt them, because what happens is they ridicule the Word and they make light of the Word. Sometime in their life they are going to need the truth, but they have already put it down. They have already trampled it under foot, and it is not going to produce in their life.

Now, look at verse seven. *"Ask, and it shall be given you; seek, and you shall find; knock, and it shall be opened unto you: For every one that asketh receiveth; and he that seeketh findeth; and to him that knocketh it shall be opened."* Notice this verse does not end with "if it be thy will". The scripture does not say that, but that is how we have read it. He said, *"Ask, and it shall be given you ... Ask, and it shall be given you ..."*

"I know that is what the Bible says, Charles, but you never know what God is going to do. He might heal this one and probably will not heal anybody else for twenty more years. Because you never know what God is going to do. Because God sees things that we do not see and He's got a bigger picture than we have. He realizes and He sees and He looks down through the eons of time and realizes that if I had that thing it would probably destroy me. So that is why God did not give it to me."

I remember several years ago a little child died and people were trying to reconcile it in their minds. They were trying to find an answer that they could live with for the rest of their lives. I heard someone say to the family that, "God in His wisdom looked down through the eons of time and saw that one day that little child was going to turn from Him so He took the child now." All I could think of when I heard that was if that was how God did things, none of us would be alive today. He would have destroyed all of us before we were even born.

HOW MUCH MORE

Matthew 7:8-11, *"For every one that asketh receiveth; and he that seeketh findeth; and to him that knocketh it shall be opened. Or what man of there of you, whom if his son ask bread, will he give him a stone?"* If your child asks you for a piece of bread would you give him a rock? If your child asks you for a piece of fish would you give him a snake?

"If ye then, being evil, know how to give good gifts unto your children, how much more (Mark those three words in your Bible, we're talking about prayer.) *shall your Father which is in heaven give good things* (What does He give? Good things.) *to them that ask him? Therefore all things whatsoever ye would that men should do to you, do ye even so to them: for this is the law and the prophets."* You see what He said there in verse eleven, *"If ye then, being evil, know how to give good gifts unto your children, how much more shall your Father which is in heaven give good things to them that ask him* (give good things to them that ask Him, give good things to them that ask Him)?" How much more? How much more? We cannot measure how much more God will give to us. Paul said in Ephesians 3:20, *"Now unto him that is able to do exceeding abundantly above all that we ask or think ..."*

[margin note: carnal]

I want you to get this next thought down into your heart so you can have an effective prayer life as Jesus said in John 15:7-8, *"If you abide in me, and my words abide in you, ye shall ask what ye will, and it shall be done unto you. Herein is my Father glorified, that ye bear much fruit ..."* God receives glory

[margin note: action]

when you and I, the members of the body of Christ, pray and receive answers to our prayers. That is when God receives glory.

Oftentimes I have heard people pray and say, "Father in the name of Jesus we need to have this done but we know or we realize that this might not be the way you want to do it. And so if it doesn't get done, that is alright. And we will just accept your will. Thy will be done, oh Lord, not ours." That sounds good but they are committing one of the greatest mistakes in prayer. They did not decide what they wanted.

"But, Charles, what I want may be wrong." Possibly. That is why at times you should go to the Lord in prayer before you ever petition Him. I do this quite often when I have a situation that I need to pray about that is not pressing. There are times when we have 30, 60 or 90 days before something must be done. That is a good opportunity to do a little homework, particularly if you are not clear what action to take.

Oftentimes I pray like this — "Lord Jesus you are the head of the church and I am a member of your body. Give me insight here. You know what needs to be done in this situation." Once He shows me the path I should take I then go to the Father and say, "Father, in the name of Jesus, by the direction of your Son, I pray and I'm asking you to accomplish this thing and I receive it done in the name of Jesus. Amen."

Praise God! You see that produces faith in your heart. It is God's will to answer prayer.

But prayer is not complaining. Amen? "God, I need this, God, I want that. Do something about that person. I do not like this situation. God, you need to go here, God, you need to go there." Realize, God is not holding out on you in prayer.

CHAPTER II
STEPS TO ANSWERED PRAYER

I want to give you some things I call steps to answered prayer. This is not something that you do one, two, three, four, five, six, seven and when you reach seven, bells begin to ring and angels come down and deliver what you prayed for. That is not what I am talking about. These are truths you need to know in order to get answers in prayer.

1. DECIDE WHAT YOU WANT

Do not pray in generalities. Be as specific as you can. Decide what you want.
The reason why I say this is because making a decision what you want keeps you from becoming double-minded, which can be very dangerous to a Christian. James chapter one says for a double-minded man not to think he shall receive anything he asks for from the Lord. <u>Decide what you want and then stick with it.</u>
You say, "Charles, if after I pray I discover that I actually needed more than what I prayed for or I needed something in addition to or maybe something even better than what I thought I did — does that mean I can't change my prayer?" Sure you can change your prayer. You can go to the Father and say, "Father, in the name of Jesus you know I prayed that and praise God I believe I received it and I believe you have given it to me, but during the course of standing on Your Word I have discovered that instead of a hundred dollars I actually need a hundred and fifty. So I am just revising this petition and I thank you for it."
You may say that sounds like being double-minded. No, this is what double-minded sounds

like, "Father, I ask you to give me $100.00 but I'll take $50.00 — actually $25.00 would be nice. Dear God, I'd be happy if I just got $10.00. I don't deserve any of it. Maybe I shouldn't ask God for $100.00 —you know that is a lot of money. Dear me, I probably just shouldn't ask God. Anyway He probably doesn't even want to give it to me. What makes me think He will? He doesn't want to give it to me. Dear me, who do I think I am?" That's double-minded.

Decide what you want. Make up your mind. Stick your heels in the ground and don't back down. Decide what you want.

2. FIND THE WORD OR GOD'S PROMISE THAT COVERS THE AREA THAT YOU ARE PRAYING ABOUT

Base your prayer on God's Word. Get some scriptures to base your prayer on. There are promises to cover every area of need in your life. There are all kinds of promises when it comes to healing. There are all kinds of promises when it comes to financial prosperity. There are all kinds of promises when it comes to wisdom.

Find something you can sink your spiritual teeth into. Something you can hold onto. Find a promise that covers the area of the need — and find more than one.

3. ASK GOD FOR WHAT YOU WANT AND DO NOT BE EMBARRASSED

"Oh but Charles, it embarrasses me to talk to God about this." Why does it embarrass you? Do you think you don't deserve it? If so then you might want to do a study on righteousness. Is your heart condemning you because you have sin in your life? Then confess it and get it out of your life.

Remember, according to John 16:23, you must address your petition to the Father in the name of Jesus. *"And in that day ye shall ask me nothing. Verily, verily, I say unto you, Whatsoever ye shall ask the Father in my name, he will give it you."* Not to the Holy Spirit, in the name of Jesus. Not to Jesus — you pray to the Father.

4. WHEN YOU PRAY, BELIEVE THAT YOU RECEIVE

Number 4 is based on Mark 11:24 and Matthew 21:22. Jesus said, *"And all things whatsoever ye ask in prayer, believing, ye shall receive."* Mark 11:24 says, *"...what things so ever ye desire, when ye pray, believe that ye receive them, and ye shall have them."*

When do you believe that you receive? When you pray. "I believe that I have it after I see it." Then you are not going to get it. There is no faith in that. You believe you receive when you pray.

Now that is so simple. You see, prayer has two pillars — trust and faith. Trusting God and believing His Word. Now those two points have the same foundation — love. When you know that God loves you then you know He will answer your prayer.

Believe that you receive when you pray.

The next step — now this one you may or may not have to do depending upon the things you have prayed about.

5. CAST DOWN IMAGINATIONS THAT ARE CONTRARY TO WHAT YOU PRAYED

II Corinthians 10:4-5 says, *"For the weapons of*

our warfare are not carnal, but they are mighty through God to the pulling down of strongholds; Casting down imaginations, and every high thing that exalteth itself against the knowledge of God, and bringing into captivity every thought to the obedience of Christ."

Do not allow thoughts to go through your mind unattended that are contrary to what you prayed. Speak God's promise to the thought. You must cast those imaginations down.

6. MEDITATE ON THE WORD

The next thing you need to do is meditate on God's promises. Find out what the promises say. The word meditate means to "revolve in the mind and to speak to yourself in a low tone of voice." Train yourself to think on God's promises. Robert Tilton says he likes to chew God's Word mentally. I like that.

Also, as opportunities arise confess God's Word to yourself in a low tone of voice. By meditating on God's Word you will begin to see yourself with your prayer answered. Your inner image is very important in your prayer life.

Meditate on God's promises. Begin to see yourself with it.

7. SPEND TIME THANKING GOD

Spend time thanking God. Thanksgiving is the track upon which faith carries its mighty load. Thanksgiving is not for God. It is for you. It keeps the reality of answered prayer alive in your heart. Thanksgiving keeps the devil from talking you out of it.

Sometimes in prayer, in some areas, you will pray about something and there will be a time period before it comes to pass. Have you ever had that experience? I have. You may be in it right now. Do you know what that time is called? Growing time. The Word is growing in your heart. First the blade, then the ear, then the full corn in the ear (Mark 4:26-29).

We know from Mark 4:14-18 that Satan comes against us to try and steal the seed of God's Word out of our heart. So don't let him! He will come and tell you, "You're not going to get it. What makes you think you're going to have that. That's too much, that's too big. How is God going to get that to you? You don't have that much money. You're too sick. That situation has gone too far, it is too bad." He will tell you all those things and many more.

What are you going to do? This is what I have done and it works for me. I spend time in thanksgiving. "Father, I thank you in the name of Jesus for meeting my need. I have it now. My needs are met. The Word is working in my life and on my behalf. I thank you Father God that you have supplied my needs exceedingly and abundantly above all I can ask or think. I am not wanting or lacking in anything, because the Lord is my shepherd. I do not want. You have caused your Word, Father God, to be manifested towards me — you have caused the angels to go forth and bring it to me. I thank you Father that I am not wanting or lacking in any area because my God is my source of supply. His arm is not shortened and His ear is not deaf and He has stretched forth His hand and caused great things to happen to me. I thank you today Father, in the name of Jesus, that everything I set my hand to do is blessed of God and is caused to prosper. I cannot fail in anything I do. The devil is a liar and I don't believe anything he tells me because the Lord has done exceedingly and abundantly above all I can ask or think." You see that is the way you do it. It's simple to do and the more you do it the stronger you become.

Remember, thanksgiving is not for God. It is for you. It strengthens you. It keeps your faith alive in your heart. It keeps you strong in the Word. It keeps your faith working.

Don't ever allow yourself to say things like, "Well, I guess we're not going to get it — I guess we prayed wrong, I guess we did this wrong, I guess we did that wrong." Don't guess. Know! If you prayed wrong then repent and pray again. But do not let the devil talk you out of it either. Depend upon the ministry of the Lord Jesus Christ and the ministry of the Holy Spirit to help you in prayer. Remember that Jesus is praying for you and the Holy Spirit will pray through you in other tongues.

There is more working for you in prayer than against you.

CHAPTER III
BUILDING
A PRAYER HABIT

Now oftentimes believers have thought of prayer as a responsibility, as a duty, as something that must be done because we are supposed to do it.

I remember when I became a Christian, I started fellowshipping with other Christian people. They told me that what I needed to do in order to stay a good Christian was to read my Bible and pray. Have you ever heard that before? You need to read your Bible and pray. Well, I read my Bible and I prayed and I did not get anything out of either one. Why? Because I had no idea why I was doing either one.

We need to read the Bible and we need to pray but we need to know why and how for either to be effective.

I remember that I always got down on my knees to pray because I thought you were supposed to get down on your knees and pray. I did not say anything because I did not know what you were supposed to say. No one ever told me what prayer was. No one ever told me what I should do in prayer. The only type of prayer I had heard of was when you got in trouble and then you would hit the floor and pray and make all kinds of promises to the Lord, that if He would just get you out of trouble this time you would really straighten up. And generally what you would pray was, "Oh God, I am sorry. Oh, don't let them get me. I repent. I tell you, Lord, if you get me out of this I will never do this again."

That is all I knew about prayer. It was a real revelation to me when I finally became involved with people who had a different attitude about prayer. They had a winning attitude about prayer and when they prayed, they prayed powerfully.

Have you ever heard someone pray powerfully?

POWER IN PRAYER

The ingredient that makes prayer powerful is the Word of God. That's right — praying God's Word.

The first time I heard someone pray God's Word was in a teaching seminar I was attending right after I was baptized in the Holy Ghost. That night the man who prayed over the offering used Luke 6:38 as the basis for his prayer. I will never forget how excited I became when I heard him pray. I had never heard anything like it. Previously, the praying I had heard was based upon two areas, trying to get God to get you out of trouble and asking Him to forgive you of sin. Those were the main areas of prayer I had heard. Oh, I heard people pray at ball games. "Lord, bless these people that nobody gets hurt today. Amen. Now go out and kill those bums." But that night at the seminar I began to realize there was more to prayer than I had been led to believe.

I then began to read books on prayer. I began to study prayer. I realized that I did not know anything about prayer. Until that time prayer was a mere religious form to me. I am convinced that of all the things in the Bible that we as Christians have put into a religious text, the one that has hurt us most has been prayer.

Putting prayer into a religious context has hurt the body of Christ the most because prayer is our contact with God. It is that thing that He has given us that we use to appropriate His power. Prayer is the thing that God uses to bring His power into manifestation. All Christian endeavor — I don't care how noble the cause, I don't care how great the vision, if it is not undergirded with prayer it will fail.

A lot of people have substituted hard work for prayer. I am not saying that we are not supposed to work hard. We are supposed to work hard. But what I am saying is that many people, especially ministers, have substituted hard work for prayer. They believe that through programs or committees or ideas backed with many hours of work they will see their churches or organizations grow. I believe in programs in the church and sometimes committees can be helpful, but the thing that makes churches grow is prayer.

Prayer is what makes people grow.

THE PRAYER HABIT

Now I want us to talk on the subject of building a prayer habit. Prayer should be as natural to you as breathing and as enjoyable as eating. "Charles, I really like to eat." I know you do, that is why I said what I said. It should be as natural to you as breathing. You should not even have to think about praying.

E.W. Kenyon said to see a need is a call to prayer. You should not even have to think about praying —it should be as natural as breathing. When something comes up the first thing that comes to your mind should be "let's pray". And you should only pray when you are expecting to get results; when you expect for something to change.

I remember when I was a little boy we used to have a plaque in my house that belonged to my dad when he was a little boy. It said, "Prayer Changes Things". I remember I would look at it and think about those words. Sitting in my room, I thought about it — "prayer changes things". But no one I saw expected anything to happen when they prayed. If something did happen, they were more surprised than anyone.

PROPER ATTITUDE

Most people's concept of prayer is that prayer is something you are supposed to do — you are not supposed to understand it. You are not supposed to see anything come about. It is just something God said, so you better do it. But that is not what prayer is all about.

Prayer is an invitation from God for you to come and fellowship with Him. It can be as natural as breathing. When you get up in the morning you do not have to remind yourself to breathe. You do it naturally. And you probably do not have to remind yourself to eat either. Your body will do that. I am making fun of that because I am making a point. I eat because I enjoy eating. I don't apologize for it. I pray because I enjoy praying and I do not apologize for it.

Your attitude towards prayer is formed by the things you have heard about prayer — good or bad. Do you see prayer as something to be enjoyed or something to be avoided? Your attitude will determine your effectiveness and your effectiveness will affect your attitude. The knowledge that you have of God's Word will dictate the effectiveness of your prayer life. Faith cometh by hearing and hearing by the Word of God. If all you have heard is that God only answers some prayers, if it is according to His will, then that is all you will get.

Prayer is a means that God has provided for us to labor together with Him in the fields of harvest.

Prayer is simply talking things over with God, getting His views, His will, His plans, and carrying out those plans with His grace, His ability and His wisdom.

Prayer is a habit that is born out of your will. You need to develop a prayer habit.

BELIEVING PRAYER

Prayer is something that you decide to do and the key part of prayer is faith. It is believing prayer that works. Do you understand that?

"Well, we're going to pray. You know we hope something happens but if it doesn't we'll understand because you never know God's will." No, family, if that is the way you are going to pray don't even bother. You are just using up good oxygen and I am convinced that God does not hear that kind of praying.

There are a lot of prayers that God never hears; prayers that are not prayed according to His Word.

I was listening to a man on a tape one time and he told this story. He said a young man came to him one day while he was doing a meeting in a church. This young man came to the parsonage where the preacher was staying and knocked on the door. The preacher answered and said, "What can I do for you?" And he said, 'As you know I have been attending the meetings and I would like for you to agree with me in prayer concerning something." The preacher said, "Well, what is it?" The young man said, "Do I have to tell you?" And the preacher said, "Yes, you must tell me so I will know what I am believing for." The young man hesitated and then said, "Alright, what I want you all to pray for is that God will give me this other man's wife." The preacher could not believe his ears. He looked at this man and said, "I'm not going to pray for that." The young man said, "You're not?" The preacher answered, "No, I'm not going to pray for that." The young man replied, "Well, the Bible says whatsoever things you desire ..." The preacher interrupted, "Yes, but the Bible also says covet not thy neighbor's wife."

God is not going to answer that type of prayer. That young man can pray all day long. He can pray to the Father. He can pray in the name of Jesus. He can fast until he dies and God is not going to answer that prayer because it is not in accordance with His will.

How do we know the will of God? His Word is His will. God's will and His Word do not contradict. They are one and the same.

I John 5:14, 15 reveals to us that we must pray according to God's will in order for our prayers to be heard. When you know that your request is in accordance with God's will you do not have any trouble with faith.

It is believing prayer that works in your life.

Faith will lead you where reason will not walk. Reason will stay down in the valley; faith will climb the mountain.

A LIFE OF PRAYER

You need to develop a life of prayer.

I remember when I started developing a prayer life. I would begin to pray and I would run out of things to say in five minutes. I would pray for everybody I knew and every problem they had in two minutes. The extent of my prayer life was, "God help my mama, God help my wife, God help me, God help the government, God help my church, God I need more money. Thank you." It did not take me long to cover all the bases. Now it takes a lot longer to pray about those things.

I have observed something very interesting that I

want to share with you along these lines. When we have a situation come into our lives (I have done it and you have done it and there is nothing wrong with it, but I am using it to bring out a point) unconsciously we are led towards and call upon people we know have active prayer lives. Isn't that right?

I remember when I learned that I could pray and God would hear me and answer me just as well as if I got Brother Copeland to pray — absolutely amazing. I always thought that if I could just get Brother Copeland to pray for me something would happen. I was drawn towards him and I unconsciously wanted to call upon him because I knew he had an active prayer life — an effective prayer life. We are drawn towards those people.

I am using this to make the point that there is nothing wrong with asking for help. Do not ever be ashamed of asking somebody for help in prayer. It is not a sign of weakness. It is a sign of intelligence. I am serious. Do not flounder around and remain strapped to something that you cannot handle with your own faith. Find someone who can help you. Reach out and get some help.

As you develop an active prayer life you will begin to see people coming to you for help. When people who at one time would not have anything to do with you discover that you have an active prayer life they will find something to do with you. People are desirious of someone who can tap into the supernatural power of God.

You cannot spend time in prayer and in fellowship with God and be unaffected by it. People of prayer do not pray all day long and come out of their house an hour in the evening and then go back into drudgery and prayer. I am talking about people who have a disciplined prayer life; who take time every day and spend it in prayer.

Prayer is not just petitioning. Prayer is talking things over with the Lord.

THE INTERNAL EFFECTS

You find somebody who has a disciplined prayer life and there is a quietness about them. There is an unshakeableness about their faith that you can sense. There is a peace in their lives which they get from God. His quietness, His unshakeableness, His peace overflows into them during the time of prayer. When you find these kind of people, they have a spiritual fragrance about them. You enjoy being in their presence.

I have discovered that people of prayer are slow to speak. They do not run off at the mouth all the time. They listen. But when they talk people listen, because they have something to say. I have also found that they are slow to judge. They are also quick to love, quick to help. Their hearts are tender and there is (and I do not know another way to say it to you than this) a holy calmness about them. You can sense it.

VALUABLES OF PRAYER

Prayer is valuable because you get to be in the presence of God and fellowship with Him. Another thing that makes prayer valuable is answers.

"Well now, Charles, I don't know about that." The only reason you say that is because you look at prayer religiously. You look at it as a spiritual, religious obligation, a slavish duty that God has given you to perform whether you like it or not. So when you go into prayer you are bored and God is happier than you are when the time is up. We should expect answers when we pray.

Joshua stood in the valley of Ajalon and spoke to the sun and the moon and told them to stop by the name of the almighty God. All of the universe froze right there and refused to move until Joshua was through.

Study the prayers of Jesus — the simplicity with which He prayed over the five loaves and two fishes with 15,000 people sitting down in front of Him. The Bible says He just looked towards heaven and thanked God and just blessed it. He then had it divided among the people. In John the seventeenth chapter He prays that magnificent prayer of intercession for you and me that still is in effect today.

We must understand that prayer does not fit into one little formula. There are times when you pray a very simple prayer and that is all you have to do. There are other times when we must stand before the throne of the almighty God and stand in the gap for somebody. You may be there for hours or days praying and interceding and fighting the battle that Satan has brought on a family or institution. There are times when we must do that.

Prayer is not a little patented, cut and dry formula where we shoot a little deal up to heaven and God sprinkles magic dust on it and everything becomes alright. Prayer undoubtedly changes things and the prayer of faith works. But, sometimes you must pray the prayer of faith and do warfare against the onslaught of the enemy and sometimes that takes more than three minutes.

There have been times when people have called me for prayer, and after I had prayed for them the thing we had prayed about stayed in my spirit and in my mind. I would continue to thank God for them and hold that situation before the throne of God and fight on their behalf. There are times when we must fight a demonic attack that comes against people.

It seems that everybody wants a formula. But we must remember that there are different kinds of prayer that work with different rules.

I am going to ask you a question and I want you to be truthful with me. Have you ever prayed about something and did not receive the answer you prayed for? I would venture to say that we could go to just about all Christians and many of them, if they were honest, would say, "I prayed and nothing happened." What about that?

That is hard to swallow especially in the light of scriptures like John 16:23 where Jesus said, *"And in that day ye shall ask me nothing ... Whatsoever ye shall ask the Father in my name, he will give it to you."* Mark 11:24 says, *"...what things soever you desire, when ye pray, believe that ye receive them, and ye shall have them."* Matthew 7:7, Jesus said, *"Ask, and it shall be given you; seek, and ye shall find; knock, and it shall be opened unto you."*

"Well, I asked the Father in the name of Jesus and I did not receive. How come?"

Some people would have you to think it was not God's will to give it to you and that is why you did not receive. No. That is not right. That is not right at all. That is not even close to right. Family, God is not the problem in prayer. But we have thought, "We must bombard the gates of heaven. We must grab hold of the horns of the altar." Why? Now, granted there are times of intercession when we stay in prayer for a long time and we do not move until the answer comes because of the situation that has presented itself.

God is not the problem in prayer.

CHAPTER IV
THE ENEMIES OF PRAYER

Many people do not receive in prayer because of what I call the enemies of prayer. In this chapter we are going to talk about these enemies of prayer.

The first enemy we will talk about is LACK OF KNOWLEDGE OF WHO AND WHAT WE ARE IN CHRIST JESUS. Many people treat prayer as a situation where they must stay before God and cry so long and so loud that He finally gives them what they want just to get rid of them. Have you ever been around a child who has learned how to do that with his parents? He has learned to cry, scream, holler and throw himself down on the floor and make enough noise and harrass them long enough until they finally give him what he wants.

THE OLD TRICK

A lot of Christian people have tried to use that same method with God, but God does not fall for that old trick. He is smarter than that.

No, it is not bawling and squalling and hollering and screaming and crying and making noise and threatening and begging that will move God. We should have figured that out by now. People do not know who they are and what they are in Christ Jesus, and because of that they do not know they are sons of God. (John 5:1) They do not know they can come into the throne room of grace boldly and obtain mercy and find grace to help in time of need. (Hebrews 4:16) They do not know that God looks upon them as His own children, as heirs of God and joint heirs of Jesus Christ. (Romans 8:14, 16) Those things are not realities in their life and because of that they deal with God as if they were still separated from Him.

You must find out who you are in Christ and the only way you are going to find that out is to open up your Bible and read it.

If you do not know who you are, then you are going to act like a beggar. You may say, "God knows I have need of this, why doesn't He just do it?" Because God is not going to force Himself on you in any way at any time. God does not want puppets. He does not want people who walk around with no will of their own, with no choice. He wants children. You must know who you are and what you are in Christ Jesus.

Another enemy of prayer is that PEOPLE ARE IGNORANT OF WHAT TRUE BELIEVING IS. So often people try to base believing on a feeling.

Now, we know that faith is the foundation of prayer. Apart from faith, you can pray all day long, and you are not going to get an answer.

Mark 11:24, *"Therefore I say unto you, what things soever ye desire, when you pray, believe that ye receive them, and ye shall have them."*

When do you believe that you receive? When you pray! Not when you get it. If you are going to wait to believe until you receive, you are not going to receive. You must believe that you receive when you pray.

GOOSEBUMPS

People try to do all kinds of things to get their believing up. They think that they have believed when they feel a certain way. "Well, I'll tell you this morning I was in there praying, glory to God, and I asked God to give me this, and I tell you I know He heard me. I know He heard me. I know I've got it, because I got fourteen goosebumps on my left arm when I prayed. Glory to God, I tell you the goosebumps were so strong in my prayer closet this morning. I know God heard my prayer."

If it is goosebumps that gives you the confidence that God heard you, I will invest in buying you a block of ice that you can sit on every time you pray. You will get goosebumps with that block of ice. Nowhere in the Bible does it say, "Therefore what things soever you desire, when you pray, believe that you receive them when you get goosebumps, and you shall have them." If your entire relationship with God is based upon your feelings, you are going to be so shallow in the kingdom of God that you are never going to amount to anything. Feelings are so fickle; they are so easily changed; they are so easily influenced.

If you are looking for feelings in the spiritual realm and in your relationship with God, the devil will lead you down a primrose path that you may never recover from, because he is the god of this world. He is the god of the feeling world. Deceit trick

Now, we thank God for feelings when they come. But whether they come or not, that is not our evidence that God has heard us. There are times when I pray that the glory of God rises up in my heart, and I know that God is listening to me. There are other times when I pray that I have no feelings at all. But that is alright, because believing is not a feeling.

Do you know what believing is? Believing is acting on God's Word. You act on what the Word says.

Now, if feelings come, great. If a feeling does not come, great. It does not make any difference one way or the other. I am spending a lot of time on this because we as Christians have a feeling religion. "I feel saved, therefore I must be. I feel close to the Lord; I must be close to him. Did you feel the Holy Ghost?" We must quit basing our faith on our feelings. They will let us down everytime.

(3) Another enemy of prayer is WRONG CONFESSIONS AND WRONG CONVERSATIONS. I have found this to be especially true in the area of the family. Almost everywhere I go to conduct a teaching seminar, somebody will walk up to me while I am there and grab my hand and say, "Brother Charles, I've got a no-good-for-nothing son. He is a worthless bum. Would you please pray for him every day until he comes to the Lord?" No. I tell people that. I say no. They look at me with a shocked look on their face. I am not going to stand there and tell them I am going to pray for their child when I know that I'm not. I will forget them two days later. I will not even think about it anymore. I have other people to pray for, other things on my mind. Yes, I am concerned about that boy. I care about him, but I tell you right now, nine times out of ten I could pray for their son everyday, all day long until Jesus comes back to the earth and it would not do any good, because his parents were constantly saying, "That boy is a no-good-for-nothing bum that will never amount to anything. He will probably end up in prison; he is just a worthless piece of no-good-for-nothing." You can pray all day long, but when you leave your prayer closet and somebody asks, "How is your son?" and your reply is that he is a worthless no-good-for-nothing, you have just negated all the praying everybody has been doing. Why? Because you believe the negative things you are saying more than what you have been praying in your prayer room.

If you believe what you pray, you will change what you say. Your heart is always going to tell on you. That's right, your heart is always going to tell on you.

Jesus said that out of the abundance of your heart your mouth speaketh. (Matthew 12:34) Your heart will give you away. Your heart will always give you away, because your tongue is tied directly to your spirit. When you have prayed about something, do not say things that are contrary to what you want or what you prayed about.

You have got to watch your mouth. The Bible says that life and death is in the power of the tongue (Prov. 18:21). Your life today is a direct product of the words you have spoken in the past.

"I don't believe in that confession teaching." It does not make any difference whether you believe in it or not because it is working for you or it is working against you every day of your life.

God has revealed this law to us so we can line our lives up with it instead of living in ignorance and working against it all the days of our lives. Your words must be in agreement with what you prayed for.

Another enemy of prayer is MENTAL ASSENT. Mental assent is when somebody accepts God's Word as true but does not act on it.

"Yes, I believe the Bible is true. I believe the Bible is the Word of God, but..." The word "but" is the key word in a mental assenter's vocabulary. "Yes, I know the Bible says I am healed, but..." They mentally assent to the Word of God; they mentally agree that the Word is true, but they do not act on it.

Another enemy of prayer is that PEOPLE THINK THAT LONG HOURS AND MUCH REPETITION IS WHAT GETS ANSWERS.

Psalm 127:1, *"Except the Lord build the house, they labour in vain that build it: except the Lord keep the city, the watchman waketh but in vain. It is vain for you to rise up early, to sit up late, to eat the bread of sorrows for he giveth his beloved sleep."* How many times I have thought that what I needed to do was to pray all night long and then God would answer me.

The amount of time you spend praying is not what makes prayer work. Faith is what makes prayer work. Now, I have stayed up all night and prayed, but I got the answer the first five minutes I was praying. The rest of the time I spent in thanksgiving and praying for other people. There are times when you will pray for a long time, particularly in the area of intercession. We will study intercessory prayer later in this book and we will discuss that in greater detail.

You should spend a lot of time in prayer, but do not think that because you prayed three hours today your prayers are guaranteed to be answered. God is not impressed with how long you pray.

Do not put your confidence in the amount of time you spend in prayer. Put your confidence in the integrity of God's Word.

CHAPTER V
KINDS OF PRAYER

Ephesians 6:10, *"Finally, my brethren, be strong in the Lord, and in the power of His might. Put on the whole armor of God, that ye may be able to stand against the wiles of the devil. For we wrestle not against flesh and blood but against principalities, against powers, against the rulers of the darkness of this world, against spiritual wickedness in high or in heavenly places: Wherefore* (or because we wrestle not against flesh and blood but we do wrestle against principalities and powers and the rulers of the darkness of this world and wicked spirits in high and heavenly places) *take unto you the whole armor of God, that ye may be able to withstand in the evil day, and having done all to stand.* (The literal Greek text here says "and having overcome all, to stand.") *Stand therefore, having your loins girt about with truth, and having on the breastplate of righteousness; and have your feet shod with the preparation of the gospel of peace; Above all, taking the shield of faith, wherewith ye shall be able to quench all the fiery darts of the wicked. And take the helmet of salvation, and the sword of the Spirit, which is the Word of God: Praying always with all prayer and supplication in the spirit, and watching thereunto with all perseverance and supplication for all saints."*

One translation says, "praying always with all different types of prayer." Another translation says, "praying always with all different kinds of prayer." I like the Goodsby translation which says, "Use every kind of prayer and entreaty and at every opportunity pray in the spirit." He said use every kind of prayer and entreaty and at every opportunity pray in the spirit.

We have learned that prayer is not just telling God the problem. God knows the problem. Hebrews the fourth chapter says that everything is naked and open before His eyes. God knows the problems. Your telling God what is wrong is not going to change what is wrong. If God's knowing what was wrong would change it then nothing would stay wrong for very long. Amen?

In fact, prayer is not so much telling God the problem as it is receiving the answer. That is what prayer is designed to do; prayer was designed to change things.

Now, prayer is an interesting subject because a lot of people think they know what prayer is. They think that they understand prayer and they think they know everything there is to know about prayer. But if they sat down and got really honest with themselves — if they received an answer to 30% of their prayers they would be excited. If they received an answer to 30% of their prayers they probably could not sleep at night. I know people who pray for years and years and years and years and maybe see one answer come about.

WHY PRAYERS ARE NOT ANSWERED

All of us have had prayers that have not been answered. I have prayed prayers that have not been answered. I am not proud of it but I want us to talk about it. Let us bring it out into the open. We need to be honest with each other. It is time for the Christian community to quit sweeping these things under the rug. It is time to pull them out here and find some answers.

One reason why people do not receive answers to prayer is because they pray the wrong kind of prayer. The Bible says use every kind of prayer. There is more than just one kind of prayer. Now, they all operate under the same premise; the same foundation is true in every prayer. You pray to the Father in the name of Jesus and you believe you receive when you pray; but, remember, there are different kinds of prayer.

Goodsby said once again, to use every kind of prayer and entreaty and at every opportunity pray in the spirit. Use every kind of prayer.

Sometimes people do not receive from God because of the things that are in their hearts. The book of Psalms says that if you regard iniquity in your heart God will not hear you when you pray. That is right. That is what it says. We cannot just bump along in our merry little lives doing whatever we jolly well please and just sin any time we would like to, and then stop when we get in trouble and say, "Hey, God" and the power of God comes upon the situation. Life does not work that way.

You may ask, "Do I have to earn God's blessing?" No. You do not have to earn anything from God but you are going to live like God said you are supposed to live or He is not going to play ball with you. Is that blunt enough for you? I cannot put it any plainer than that. You cannot live in sin, doing things contrary to the law of God when He has dealt with you and told you to repent, but you do not obey. Then you get in a tight spot and turn around and expect God to fix everything — make everything hunky-dory —because He is not going to do it.

If you regard iniquity in your heart, if there is sin in your heart and you know it and you refuse to repent of it, and you will not change your actions and you continue to live in that state of sin — I'm telling you right now, God is not going to listen to you when you pray. He is not going to do it.

You may say, "Do we have to be perfect then before God will listen to us?" What do you think? Do you think you have to be perfect before God will hear you? Have you ever received an answer to a prayer? Well, that proves it — you do not have to be perfect. Amen?

You do not have to be perfect to get answered prayer, but I will tell you what you have to do; you have to walk in the light of the Word that you have received. Now you may say, "I know people who are living in sin and God answers their prayer." But do they know they are living in sin? The apostle Paul wrote in the book of Romans and said that before the Word comes there is no knowledge of sin. There are things people do, but they do not know those things are wrong. They may have even been told that it was alright to act that way by their church. Then they start listening to the spirit of God and He begins telling them things — doesn't He? He starts telling them to stop acting certain ways and to stop doing certain things. They are then faced with a new decision — whether to obey or not to obey. If they choose to go ahead then they have made the decision to sin.

"But Charles, I just cannot stop! It is too hard." You can stop with God's help. I have known men who have walked away from ten to fifteen years of drug and alcohol addiction after simply bowing their knees and praying a simple prayer such as, "God, I want to quit and I believe that you will help me." Then they turn around and walk off and never touch it again. If they can do that, you can quit whatever is in your life. Now granted, it took the spirit of God to give them strength, but getting Him to help is not a problem. We do not have to twist His arm to make Him do anything. We do not have to sit around and beg the Holy Ghost to help us. He is here to help us.

YOU CAN ONLY DO SO MUCH

Oftentimes people get frustrated in praying for other people. Let me tell you something about praying for other people; your prayer can only go so far. It can only do so much. In fact, you cannot make people receive — did you know that?

I prayed for a man one time in a hospital room. He was dying. The doctor had just been in before I got there and told him there was no hope. They were going to send him home to die. There was no hope —he was dying of incurable cancer. They really had no idea how long he would live. The family did not call us to pray. Somebody else who was involved asked if my wife and I would come up and pray. I do not like situations like that. This man and his wife were very polite and very nice but they did not believe that anything could be done. They didn't have any hope. Before we prayed for them all they were talking about was getting out of the hospital and going somewhere for some special treatment. When we prayed, that was all they could think about. I am not criticizing them. I understand desperation. But I will never forget this as long as I live. Rochelle and I got on either side of his bed and we prayed. While we prayed for him the anointing of God fell in that room. I could feel the power of God in that room. I know the anointing of God when I feel it; I know it. I have been around enough. I know it when it comes and it was there. The power of God was there to heal that man. I reached out and set my hand on him and I prayed for him. I could feel the power of God, like electricity, flow through the back of my spine, down my arms and out my hands into his body. That man died of cancer. We told him the power of God went into his body. He would not receive it. He just looked at us. Oh, it grieves my heart. He just looked at us. Then he turned to his wife and said, "As soon as I get out of here we will go to this place and get that treatment."

Someone might say to me, "Charles, aren't you a man of faith — couldn't you pray healing into his body?" I did. "Your prayer did not work then." Sure it worked, my prayer worked.

Do you understand what I am saying? Some people will not receive. That does not mean your prayer did not work. I have prayed for people to get born again, to make Jesus the Lord of their life. They do not have to do it. You can pray and pray and pray for them but the choice is still theirs. <u>The decision still belongs to them.</u> They still make the choice and they can still choose to go the other way.

We may as well discuss this further and go into an area of some controversy. I am going to say this and you might not like it, but it is still the truth. You cannot guarantee by your prayers that your unsaved husband or wife will to get born again. You cannot do it.

"But Charles, the Bible says whatsoever thing you ask in prayer believing you shall receive." Yes, I know it says that, but your unborn-again spouse is not a "thing". You may think they are and they may act like they are, but in the mind of God, they are human and <u>they have their own will</u>.

Now, you need to pray for them and intercede for them and I will tell you what your intercession will do for them. <u>It will bring about a situation that is conducive to their getting born again.</u> But you cannot make the decision for them. I have had people come to me in various places and say, "The Bible says that whatsoever things you desire when you pray, believe you receive and you shall have them. Well, I just prayed and I believe I have received this — my husband is now in the kingdom of God and he is born again and he is going to heaven whether he likes it or not." No, he is not. <u>God is not going to transgress his will.</u>

Do you understand that? I am not trying to throw a wet blanket on your faith. I am trying to give you proper direction. I am trying to establish the right path so that you can know where you are going when you are dealing with other people.

Now, that does not mean that they are not going to receive. No, that is not true. Most people want to get better. I have prayed for a lot more people who have been healed than have not. Most people want to receive. Most people want their lives changed. But every once in a while you will come across someone who is not going to move. God will deal with him. God will talk to him. God will send His spirit to minister to him and to deal with his heart. But the final decision still belongs to that man — <u>it is still his decision</u> and he can go to hell if he wants to. God will not stop him. He will protect his right to go.

I have said this because some people think that the rules which govern prayer for their own lives can be taken and applied to somebody else. But they cannot. Now, for my wife and me and my children I can pray and believe I receive and we will receive. But even then there will come a day in my children's lives where my faith will not be as productive as it is today. Why? Because they will become accountable themselves before God. That is why it is so important that we teach them right, because some day they are going to answer for themselves.

(4) ASKING AMISS

James 4:1-3, *"From whence come wars and fightings among you? come they not hence, even of your lusts that war in your members? Ye lust, and have not: ye kill, and desire to have, and cannot obtain: ye fight and war, yet ye have not, because ye ask not. Ye ask, and receive not, because ye ask amiss, that ye may consume it upon your lusts."* He said you ask and receive not because you ask amiss that you may consume it upon your lusts.

There is an area in prayer where you can pray for something lustfully. In our day and age whenever we think of the word "lust" — we are so programmed with sex, that that is all we think of. However, that is not the only context in which that word is used. You can pray for things lustfully. You see, there is a difference between the desire of your heart and a lust of your flesh.

Psalm 37:4 says that God will give you the desires of your heart. "How do I know the difference between the desire of my heart and the lust of my flesh, Charles?" If someone prays for something because he wants to use it to impress people or to create jealousy or envy, then it is a lust of the flesh.

It is an amazing thing how Satan will take something that is the desire of your heart and will begin working on it and pervert it to where it actually becomes a lust of your flesh. "If we move into a new house then everybody will know that we are really walking with God." Do you see what I am saying? "If we get a new car then everybody at church will think that we are being spiritual with the Word of God." We know that is not true. There are all kinds of people who do not know the first thing about the Word who are moving into new houses and buying new cars. That is not a sign of spirituality, is it? That does not mean anything.

Your level of spirituality is not measured in what your net worth is. Yes, I believe in prosperity and teach that it is God's will for His people to prosper. But how much money you make or do not make is not a sign of being spiritual. The Mafia drive limousines, fly around in private jets, live in mansions, and they are far from spiritual.

Satan will, if you let him, pervert something that was a desire of your heart — that God was willing to give you — into a lust of your flesh that you want to use to make yourself look better or to intimidate others or to create jealousy or envy in someone else. The thing God had planned on giving you when it was a desire — He will end up not giving you because you are trying to get it to consume it upon your flesh. God will not give you anything that will destroy you. God has more sense than that.

But people will take a scripture like Mark 11:24 which says, *"Therefore I say unto you, What things soever ye desire, when ye pray, believe that ye receive them, and ye shall have them."* They think they can make God do things with that verse of scripture which are wrong.

Let me give you an example of that from my own life involving my earthly father. When I was sixteen years old, I could not understand why my earthly daddy would not buy me a new Corvette. He used to tell me he had the money to buy it and he could have bought me one if he wanted to. I used to say, "Daddy, I want a Corvette." I really did. I really wanted one. Oh, I had tremendous mental images of myself in that Corvette cruising around town. My dad would look at me in honesty and sincerity and say, "Son, I cannot give it to you because you cannot handle it." That was an insult. He did not mean it as an insult but I received it as that. I said, "What do you mean I cannot handle it?" He said, "You are not wise enough to know how to use a car with that much power. I would have to come unwrap you from around a telephone pole some night, and son, you mean more to me than that." Well, I did not understand that. I mean, I was sixteen years old and I knew everything. Thank the Lord my dad had sense enough not to give me that car because I would have killed myself.

All of us would agree that the Lord wants what is best for us. To repeat something I said earlier —God will not give you something that will destroy you.

THEIR OWN FREE WILL

Oftentimes when you are praying for other people you will not see your prayers answered because they have their own free will and they can choose to go the way they want to go. God will deal with them. He will talk to them. He will minister to them. He will send people to tell them the error of their way. He will show them their error. He will reveal it to them, but if they want to walk in that path they can walk in it and God will not change it. Now, that does not mean that your prayer was not heard or it did not bring effect. But what I am saying is that you cannot believe somebody else into a right way of living.

For example, let us read in Mark 10:17-25, *"And when he was gone forth into the way, there came one running and kneeled to him, and asked him, Good Master, what shall I do that I may inherit eternal life? And Jesus said unto him, Why callest thou me good? there is none good but one, that is, God. Thou knowest the commandments, Do not commit adultery, Do not kill, Do not steal, Do not bear false witness, Defraud not, Honour thy father and mother. And he answered and said unto him, Master, all these have I observed from my youth. Then Jesus beholding him loved him, and said unto him, One thing thou lackest: go thy way, sell whatsoever thou hast, and give to the poor, and thou shalt have treasure in heaven: and come, take up the cross, and follow me. And he was sad at that saying, and went away grieved: for he had great possessions. And Jesus looked round about, and saith unto his disciples, How hardly shall they that have riches enter into the kingdom of God! And the disciples were astonished at his words. But Jesus answereth again, and saith unto them, Children, how hard is it for them that trust in riches to enter into the kingdom of God! It is easier for a camel to go through the eye of a needle, than for a rich man to enter the kingdom of God."*

Notice that Jesus did not run after that young man and say, "Now wait a minute, wait a minute. I know that sounded kind of hard, let me explain myself to you. What I really meant was that if you do not want to give it all away you can just give some of it away and then I would like to have you on my personal staff." Realize, Jesus offered him apostleship, and the young man turned around and walked away. He turned his back on apostleship and Jesus let him go.

Do you know why? That was his choice. That was the decision he made. The Bible said Jesus loved him, but even in that love He could not make up his mind for him.

Let's read now in the book of Proverbs the first chapter. We are talking about why people do not get answers to prayers. Sometimes when you pray for somebody else, the prayer does not work. The first time that happens the devil will come and tell you it is your fault. Sometimes it might be your fault; maybe you did not pray correctly. There are different kinds of prayers with different kinds of rules. There are different rules that follow each type of prayer. We cannot say prayer is prayer anymore than we can say sports is sports. You cannot play baseball according to football rules. There are certain rules that follow every kind of prayer. There is the prayer of agreement, petition, confirmation, committment, intercession, and there is praying in the spirit. Most people do not know how to pray correctly and that is the reason for this book.

If I am going to take the time to pray, I want to get answers. That is why it is important to know how to pray correctly in line with God's Word. Hosea 4:6 says, *"My people are destroyed for lack of knowledge ..."* In life in general and in prayer specifically, ignorance is no excuse.

Proverbs 1:20-23 says, *"Wisdom crieth without; she uttereth her voice in the streets: She crieth in the chief place of concourse, in the openings of the gates: in the city she uttereth her words, saying, How long, ye simple ones, will ye love simplicity? and the scorners delight in their scorning, and fools hate knowledge? Turn you at my reproof: behold, I will pour out my spirit unto you, I will make known my words unto you."*

Wisdom is not hidden. God's Word is not hidden. God is not keeping His knowledge away from mankind. God wants everybody to know what is right and what is wrong. You can hear the gospel preached twenty-four hours a day, seven days a week on television and radio.

Proverbs 1:24-28, *"Because I have called and ye refused, I have stretched out my hand, and no man regarded; But ye have set at nought all my counsel, and would none of my reproof: I also will laugh at your calamity; I will mock when your fear cometh: when your fear cometh as desolation, and your destruction cometh as a whirlwind; when distress and anguish cometh upon you. Then shall they call upon me, but I will not answer ..."*

He said, *"... they will seek me early, but they shall not find me: for that they hated knowledge and did*

⑧ *not choose the fear of the Lord: they would have none of my counsel; they despised all of my reproof. Therefore shall they eat of the fruit of their own way, and be filled with their own devices. For the turning away of the simple shall slay them, and the prosperity of fools destroy them."* And then he said, *"But whoso hearkeneth unto me shall dwell safely, and shall be quiet from fear of evil."*

KEY — promises

LIFE'S GREATEST HEARTBREAK

My wife and I have talked about this several times. The greatest heartbreak in our lives is to see people come and hear and receive the Word and then for some reason or other get offended at something and turn around and walk away from everything they have learned. They turn their backs on the truth and refuse to accept it any longer. That grieves our hearts. We know where they are putting themselves. We know where they are going to end up.

When a person turns his back on the Word of God and the truth He has revealed to him, then he has set His counsel at naught. He has turned to God and called His reproof nothing. When his calamity comes the Lord is going to laugh at him. That's right. I have seen it happen more times than I care to think about. I have gone to hospital rooms before to see people with whom God has dealt all their lives. They have finally come to the end of their rope, dying of some incurable disease, and they call to ask me to come and pray. I walk into their room and there is little or nothing I can do. They are eating the fruit of their own labors. They chose that path. They wanted it and they got it.

People do not like to talk about these things. However, they are just as much in the Bible as Mark

11:24. You cannot walk contrary to God, after He has dealt with your heart through your hearing the Word, and go on wilfully, knowledgeably and purposefully setting yourself to do whatever you please, and then say, "God, help!" It does not work that way.

We are not earning the blessings of God, but I want you to read these additional verses of scripture. Isaiah 65:11-16, Psalms 1:4, Isaiah 1:15, Jeremiah 14:10-12, Micah 3:1-4, Zechariah 7:8-14 and Jeremiah 6:19 — they all basically say that when a man has heard the Word of God and refuses God's counsel that the Lord will eventually turn him over to the fruit of his own thoughts. I am telling you this because sometime you may be called into a situation to pray for somebody and nothing, absolutely nothing will happen. The reason is because the course is already set in motion and the only person who can change it is the person being prayed for. Also understand that it does not matter how far a person goes. He can always ask for forgiveness.

LIVING IN PEACE

Here is something else that keeps prayer from working — I Peter 3:5-7, *"For after this manner in the old time the holy women also, who trust in God, adorned themselves, being in subjection unto their own husbands: Even as Sara obeyed Abraham, calling him lord: whose daughters ye are, as long as ye do well, and are not afraid with any amazement. Likewise, ye husbands, dwell with them according to knowledge,* (or dwell with them according to what you know God's Word says for you to do) *giving honour unto the wife, as unto the weaker vessel, and as being heirs together of the grace of life, that your prayers be not hindered."*

Another thing that will hinder your prayers, that

will keep your prayers from being answered is strife in your home. You can pray and pray and confess and confess. You can fast until you turn into a toothpick, but your prayers will be hindered as long as you are living in strife. You could be in strife with me and I not even know it.

Strife will take you to a dead-end road. It will put you into a pit. The Bible says in James 3:16 that where there is envy and strife there is confusion and every evil work. You cannot live with strife.

Now, I realize that in some households the husband is not saved or the wife is not saved, or they may be saved but not turned on to God or His Word, and strife will arise in that household. If you are the saved person in such a house, just because your spouse is in strife does not mean that your prayers will be hindered. You can still have an effective, overcoming, spiritual life.

What Peter is talking about is two born-again, spirit-filled, hand-raising, tongue-talking, tape-listening, Bible-toting Christians who are supposed to be walking in the Word of God together. If there is strife in your household, your prayers will be hindered. You must dwell together in harmony and in peace if you want to see your prayers be effective. There is no room for strife in the Christian home.

We must realize that our children are a direct product of the way they see us live. Our children are watching us and they get an image of what marriage is from what they see at home. They get an image of what love is by watching us. If you do not want your children talking badly about people and being critical, then do not do it in front of them.

"But I'm married to someone who will not live in peace." That is not your fault, that is their problem. But you must keep your heart pure. You cannot fill your mouth with words that hurt, and sling those words out as stones against your husband or wife and then expect God's blessings to flow in your life. You must live together in harmony, and to accomplish that, sometimes you will have to just keep your mouth shut when a disagreement begins. Just grit your teeth and smile. Then begin to talk very softly, because the Bible says a soft answer turns away wrath.

A lot of people are nicer to their friends than they are to their own husbands or wives. That is sad. Do not read that verse and think, "If my husband would straighten up everything would be alright." Do not always put the blame on someone else. If your marriage needs changing, ask the Lord to change you. But whatever you do, do not start criticizing your mate. You do not win anyone to Jesus by beating them over the head. You live before them, you walk in love, you walk by faith, and they see the fruits of God's Word in your life. Nobody is perfect. Sometimes you have to admit that you are wrong.

CHAPTER VI
INTERCESSORY PRAYER

The one thing that all prayer has in common is the name of Jesus and faith. You have got to believe in the type of prayer that you are going to pray.

Now, oftentimes people will take the simple prayer of petition, which is the kind of prayer we are most familiar with, and they think that they can take the rules that govern the simple prayer of petition and bring them over into the area of intercessory prayer.

Intercessory prayer is basically standing in the gap for somebody else. Praying for someone else. Maybe you know somebody who does not know how to pray for themselves correctly. Do you know anybody like that? Maybe you know somebody who does not believe in prayer, or believes in prayer but does not know how to pray, who needs to be prayed for. For those situations, God has given us what is called intercessory prayer.

The prayer of intercession is when you intercede on behalf of someone else. However, you cannot take the rules that govern the prayer of petition that you may pray for yourself and apply those same rules to intercessory prayer and expect to see the instantaneous results in somebody else's life that you can get in your own. They are two different kinds of prayer.

The prayer of intercession is a prayer that you pray basically for other people. Now, of course, you can intercede for yourself, and the area where you have the greatest authority is in your immediate family. When you pray for somebody else, at times you can use the prayer of petition. You can pray for them as you would pray for yourself, particularly if they come to you and ask you to pray for them. When people ask me to lay my hands upon them and pray for them, they are giving me authority in their lives. They are allowing me to pray for them. But, at the same time, I cannot make them receive, any more than you can make your husband or your wife get saved, or any more than you can make your relative get born again. You can pray and intercede on their behalf. You can bring them to a point where they know they should get saved. They can find out how to get born again and their hearts will be opened and their eyes will be opened to the truth. You can do that. But the final decision is still theirs.

I have seen more people throughout the United States who have reached out and laid hold of somebody or something in prayer, and they prayed and prayed and prayed and prayed and nothing happened, and they say to me, "Oh dear me, I don't understand what is wrong." If I had time to question each one of them, I would ask them what type of prayer they were praying, how were they praying, and what were they praying. I have heard a lot of people pray things that God will never answer. The worst thing that a Christian can pray is for God to bring a person so low that they have got to look up to find Him. Demonic spirits wait for somebody to pray that type of prayer so they can move in like a flood upon that person's life and wreck havoc upon it and God will get the blame.

There is tremendous power in intercessory prayer beyond anything you and I have ever conceived of. Every great revival in the history of the church has been founded upon and undergirded by prayer. John Wesley made a statement at the end of his life. He said, "I have come to discover that God is limited as to what He can do in the earth by the prayers that men pray."

Isaiah 43:25-26, *"I, even I, am he that blotteth out*

thy transgressions for mine own sake, and will not remember thy sins. Put me in remembrance: let us plead together: declare thou that thou mayest be justified." The word "declare" literally means "set forth your case."

Now, this verse is written from the Lord to us saying, "put me in remembrance, let us plead together, set forth your case." That sounds like a lawyer standing before a judge. God is the judge of heaven and earth and He wants us to state our reasons before Him why we want something done. This is very important, particularly in the area of intercessory prayer where you are standing in the gap for someone who is in trouble and taking hold of the hand of God and bringing them together through your intercession.

Being an intercessor is not very glamorous. It can be very hard work. It can even be boring, but it is also very rewarding! A lot of people make a mistake in intercessory prayer when they ask the Lord to do things in people's lives that He cannot do for them. We need to understand that God does not have the right to move in some people's lives because they are not one of His children. They are separated from the covenant of God. They are separated from the blessings of God. They are outside of the kingdom of God. You must start with the basics. Begin with getting them saved first. Get the devil off their back. He said, "put me in remembrance, let us plead together, set forth your case, put me in remembrance, let us plead together."

Oftentimes when you start praying for someone, you need to listen to God — He might have a case. He might have something to say about the individual. We stated earlier in Proverbs 1 that in some lives God has dealt with them and finally there will come a time when He will quit dealing with them. He will quit calling them and their calamity shall come upon them and they shall cry unto Him and He will laugh at them. I have seen that happen.

REMEMBRANCERS

Isaiah 62:1, *"For Zion's sake will I not hold my peace, and for Jerusalem's sake I will not rest ..."* Who is Zion? The church is Zion. For the church's sake I will not hold my peace and for Jerusalem's sake I will not rest. Isaiah 62:6, *"I have set watchmen upon thy walls, O Jerusalem, which shall never hold their peace day nor night: ye that make mention of the Lord, keep not silence."* The word "watchmen" can be translated "remembrancers". When you first read that verse of scripture, you think that God was talking about literal guards sitting upon the walls watching for the enemy, but what He is actually talking about is intercessors — remembrancers.

Isaiah 43 said, *"Put me in remembrance: let us plead together ..."* He said, *"I have set remembrancers upon thy walls, O Jerusalem, which shall never hold their peace day nor night: ye that make mention of the Lord, keep not silence."* Isaiah 62:7, *"And give him no rest, till he establish, and till he make Jerusalem a praise in the earth."*

If you read this wrong, and a lot of people do, you will get the wrong impression and think that intercessory prayer is going before God and begging and crying. There are times in intercession when you will begin to travail. The apostle Paul in the book of Galatians likened intercessory prayer to a woman travailing in birth. Paul wrote in Galatians 4:19, *"...travail in birth again until Christ be formed in you."* There is that area of travailing in intercessory prayer, and we will study it later. He is talking to us about being the Lord's remembrancers. God wants you to remind Him of His Word.

God calls people to intercession. He calls them to stand in the gap, and take that responsibility and remind the Lord of His Word.

STANDING IN THE GAP

The greatest single example that I have ever seen of this in the Bible is found in Exodus 32:7-14. Moses was on the mountain talking with God when the nation of Israel built the golden calf down in the valley. The Bible says that God's wrath burnt hot within Him and He told Moses that He was going to destroy everyone of them but Moses, and that He was going to make a mighty nation out of him. Moses stood in the face of almighty God and said for Him to remember His covenant with Abraham, Isaac and Jacob. And the Bible says that God changed His mind. What did Moses do? He brought God into remembrance.

Another great example of intercessory prayer is Abraham on the plains of Mamre (Genesis 18:1-33) when God and the two angels came down to see Sodom and Gomorrah. While on their way to Sodom and Gomorrah they came to Abraham and he prepared a feast for them. They sat down and ate with him. As they walked towards Sodom and Gomorrah God said, *"Shall I hide from Abraham that thing which I do."* He then told Abraham that the sin of Sodom and Gomorrah was grievous and that He had come down to see for Himself how bad it was. Then Abraham stood before God and began to intercede on behalf of the others. Abraham asked the Lord if He would destroy the righteous with the unrighteous. God said, *"No."* Abraham asked that if by chance there were fifty righteous would He destroy the city for the sake of fifty righteous. And God said that for the sake of fifty righteous He would not destroy the city. Abraham then asked that if there were only forty-five would He not destroy the cities. God said that if there were only forty-five He would not destroy the cities. Abraham then slowly made the intercession all the way to only ten righteous people. If there were only ten righteous people, God said that He would not destroy the cities.

Why did Abraham stop at ten? I think he figured that between Lot and his relatives there had to have been ten righteous people. But Abraham had not seen Lot since he had moved to Sodom, and he did not know that Lot's own soul had been vexed by the wickedness as well as his own children and sons-in-law and daughters. Some of his own daughters and sons-in-law had become as wicked as the people who were living there. Abraham had no idea that it was that bad and when God saw it — you know what happened. But God in His mercy still delivered Lot and his two daughters and his wife with clear instructions to them not to look back. Lot's wife turned around because she loved the pleasures of sin more than the ways of righteousness.

Jesus said in Luke 9:62, *"...no man, having set his hand to the plough, and looking back, is fit for the kingdom of God."*

I have had people say, "Charles, I am still tempted to go back down into the bars. Boy, I really miss that." You better get ahold of that because you are looking back. What type of field are you going to plow if you are always looking back over your shoulder? You are not worthy of what God has given you, if that is the attitude that is in your heart.

Isn't it interesting that God said, *"...give me no rest."* The literal Hebrew text there says, "give him no silence." "Do we have to do that, do we have to keep plugging at God until He gets so tired of hearing us that He finally answers us?" No. What happens is that our faith is reminding Him to do these things and that faith gives Him the right to do it.

In Luke 11:5-8 Jesus gives us an illustration that is sometimes used as a model for intercessory prayer, when in reality it is not. You will see what I mean as we get into it. *"And he said unto them, Which of you shall have a friend and shall go unto him at midnight, and say unto him, Friend, lend me three loaves; For a friend of mine in his journey is come to me, and I have nothing to set before him? And he from within shall answer and say, Trouble me not: the door is now shut, and my children are with me in bed; I cannot rise and give thee. I say unto you, Though he will not rise and give him, because he is his friend, yet because of his importunity he will rise and give him as many as he needeth."* Verses 9 and 10, *"And I say unto you, ask, and it shall be given you; seek, and ye shall find: knock, and it shall be opened unto you. For every one that asketh receiveth; he that seeketh findeth; and to him that knocketh it shall be opened."*

Verses five through eight can be used to show the proper attitude in intercessory prayer except for one key word — friend. What Jesus is using here is the relationship of a friend to a friend as an illustration of how much greater our expectancy should be when we go to God who is not our friend but our Father. Is that clear to you?

He said when you are dealing with one friend for another friend then you may have to stand there and beat on the door until he gets up and gives it to you in order to get rid of you. He is using that illustration to show us that we should not have that attitude in our hearts when we intercede to our heavenly

Father. We are not dealing friend to friend, we are dealing children to Father. Children to their Father.

Now look at what else He said. *"And I say unto you, ask, and it shall be given you; seek, and ye shall find; knock, and it shall be opened unto you. For every one that asketh receiveth; and he that seeketh findeth; and to him that knocketh it shall be opened. If a son* (see, now, he has gone from a friend to a friend to an illustration of a son to a father) *ask bread of any of you that is a father, will he give him a stone ...?"* If your son comes up and asks you for a piece of bread are you going to give him a rock to eat instead? Well of course not. If he asks for a fish will you give him a serpent? If he asks for an egg will you give him a scorpion instead? Those illustrations are so absurd that Jesus did them in that very way to strike your consciousness.

A lot of people in the area of prayer will pray this way, "Now brother we are going to pray for you but we do not know how God is going to answer. We are going to pray for your wife but we do not know what God may do. He may knock her down with cancer — we don't know." That is ridiculous.

These verses of scripture prove that when you ask a father for an egg he does not give you a scorpion. This is the proper attitude to have in intercessory prayer.

PRAYING IN THE SPIRIT

I want us to talk about intercessory prayer coupled together with praying in the spirit or praying with other tongues because you cannot separate them. They work so closely together. The Bible uses the terms praying in the spirit and praying with other tongues synonymously. From a scriptural viewpoint they are one and the same.

Romans 8:26 and 27, *"Likewise the Spirit also helpeth our infirmities: for we know not what we should pray for as we ought: but the Spirit itself maketh intercession for us with groanings which cannot be uttered. And he that searcheth the hearts knoweth what is the mind of the Spirit, because he maketh intercession for the saints according to the will of God."*

There are times in our lives when we have situations and we do not know what to pray. We know how to pray; to the Father in the name of Jesus, but we may not know what to pray. At those times in our lives the Holy Spirit will help us. He will make intercession through us (verse 27) according to the will of God. In fact, the literal translation of the first part of verse 26 reads like this, *"Likewise the Spirit Himself takes hold together with us against our weaknesses."* You may not know what you need, you may not have the slightest idea what is wrong with you, but the Spirit of God does! He knows what is happening in your life. He knows what is wrong with your relatives or friends. He knows, and He wants to make intercession for and about those things and people through you.

God is crying out for intercessors. He must have people who will stand in the gap, who are willing to give of their own lives to pray for somebody else. He is crying out for people who will pray, who will be sensitive to Him. A lot of people want to be used of God. They pray, "Oh God, use me." But I am telling you, you must be available. And when that stirring comes up in your heart you must be willing to turn the television off; you must be willing to get up from bed. It happens to me all the time. Then the Holy Spirit will begin to bear witness in my heart (Romans 8:14) that He has something or someone He wants me to pray for. Sometimes He will tell me who or what He wants me to pray for. Oftentimes I never know.

You see, the role of an intercessor is not a glamorous role. The intercessor does not get his reward until he gets to heaven.

The quickest way for God to quit calling on you is to go around expecting everybody to pat you on the back and say, "Oh, how spiritual you are." God is looking for people He can depend on and trust. To be used in intercessory prayer is an important assignment that God can often use to bring about many things.

Let me give you an example. One time while I was asleep I was suddenly awakened by the Holy Spirit. I had been spending a lot of time in prayer and a lot of time in the Word and I was tuned in spiritually. The first thing I did was ask, "Lord, what is it?" He said, "I want you to get up, I have somebody I need for you to pray for." So I got up and walked into the other room. I began to walk around the room praying in the spirit. After a few minutes I said, "I do not know who to pray for, Father, and I do not know what to pray about, but you know and you know what needs to be done." I just continued walking around praying in the spirit. I prayed like that for about an hour. I did not care what time it was because I was doing something with God! I can sleep all I want when I get to heaven!

GROANING IN THE SPIRIT

Over a period of time the spirit of intercession rose up within me very strongly. I got to where I could not pray in tongues anymore. Then there came up in me a groaning; a travailing. Romans 8:26, *"...but the spirit itself maketh intercession for us with groanings which cannot be uttered."* The only thing I can liken it to is when a woman has a baby. This is a groaning that comes from down inside of you. The literal Greek text says, "groanings which cannot be expressed in articulate speech." You do not form words anymore. It is a groaning from within yourself.

Sometimes when I lay hands on people I will begin to groan like that — groaning in the spirit. Do you know what is happening then? When a woman begins to travail in birth what happens next? Something is born; something is given birth to.

When you start travailing and groaning in the spirit, then you will start seeing people get born again in church services. You will start seeing people get healed, you will start seeing people get delivered. You are giving birth to those things. They are coming about. They are happening. I am talking about intercession when you take upon yourself the feelings of a lost world.

Sometimes when I am in seminars or before services during my prayer time while I am praying for people in the meeting and interceding on their behalf for several hours, I come to a point in my spirit where I feel as though I am lost, as though I am not going to heaven. That used to scare me. But I have learned that in the role of an intercessor many times you take upon yourself the feelings of other people. When that happens now, I can hardly wait to go to the service because I know people are going to get saved. How do I know people are going to get saved? How do I know that? Because I gave birth to it during my prayer time.

Well, back to the other story. After praying in tongues for about an hour there was a note of victory in my spirit and I realized that the thing I had been praying for was done. The Lord then brought to my mind a man that I had known at one time in my life who had been very important in my spiritual growth. I had not seen him in three or four years and the Lord told me I had been praying for him and his children. He said the devil had attacked this man's children that night and had tried to destroy one of his children with sickness and disease. He said, "But I had you get up and pray for them and now the baby is healed."

One month later this man came back to El Paso and somebody else got us together. Now, a lot of water had passed under the bridge from the last time I had seen him. Primarily, I had been filled with the Holy Ghost and was now speaking with other tongues and his church did not believe in it. They believed speaking in tongues was of the devil. So when we got together all he wanted to do was argue about being filled with the Holy Ghost and speaking in tongues. I purpose to avoid getting into arguments. I do not like to argue. In fact, I refuse to argue with people. Arguing does not settle anything. All it does is create strife.

He said, "Everything I ever hear about praying in other tongues is me, me, me — it is just for you. What good does it do other people? I think you people who speak in tongues have a personality deficiency and are selfish." I just looked at him and said, "Brother, a month ago (and I related the very day and time) the Spirit of God got me out of bed and had me pray in other tongues for your children from 2:00 to 3:00 A.M. in the morning because God told me that your children were sick." His eyes got really big as he looked at me and said, "What day did you say that was?" I told him. He then looked around the room and asked the other people present, "Who told him about this?" He then said, "I do not understand this, because that very night one of my babies had a 107° fever and we could not get it down and it looked as though she was going to die. We did not know what was wrong with her and then about 3:00 in the morning the fever broke and left her and she went sound asleep and was totally well and we never had any more problems with it." I said, "Brother, that was the Spirit of God. God woke me up and had me pray for your babies." He looked at me and said, "I still do not believe in tongues." At that point, I wanted to take him outside, tie him to a tree and pray for him all night long so he could be delivered from the spirit of dumb!

There is power in intercession.

DIVINE SECRETS

I Corinthians 14:2, *"For he that speaketh in an unknown tongue speaketh not unto men, but unto God; for no man understandeth him; howbeit in the spirit he speaketh mysteries."* The Greek text there says he speaks divine secrets. Can you imagine you and God having a little secret? Isn't that dynamite?

Whenever you start praying in the spirit you are not talking to the people around you, you are talking to God. You are saying things to God that only He knows. He knew those babies were sick; I didn't.

Now, a lot of times when you start praying in the spirit and making yourself available to intercession, God will show you things that are going to happen in the future. He will reveal things to you. But do not get upset if He does not tell you what or who you have been praying for. At times, God will tell you things and at other times He will not, because it is none of your business. You do not need to know.

What you need to do is pray. God needs your intercession. He needs you to pray. "For if I pray in unknown tongues, my spirit prays." What do you pray in when your spirit prays? In an unknown tongue. How are you praying when you pray in an unknown tongue? In the spirit. This is undoubtedly one of the greatest tools that God has ever given the church. Your spirit knows things your head does not know. The Holy Spirit lives in your spirit when you are filled with the Holy Spirit and He will reveal to your spirit things that your head does not know and does not need to know.

Of course, you can pray effectively with your understanding in English or Spanish or whatever your native language may be. I do not pray in tongues all the time. Sometimes I pray in English, but the more I study about tongues, the more praying in tongues I do.

Remember what he said in Romans 8:27, *"...he maketh intercession for the saints according to the will of God."* I John 5:14 says that if we ask anything according to God's will, He hears us, and we know that if He hears us then we have the petitions we have desired from Him.

So, the key to answered prayer is to get God to hear you. How do you get God to hear you? You must pray according to His will, which can be done by praying in other tongues.

I Corinthians 14:14, *"For if I pray in an unknown tongue, my spirit prayeth, but my understanding is unfruitful."* Many people get discouraged when they pray in other tongues because their minds wander and they oftentimes end up thinking about all kinds of things. "What good is this, I am not even thinking about what I am doing?" It does not matter if your head is thinking about what you are doing. How can it think about what you are doing? You do not even know what you are praying about.

I Corinthians 14:15, *"What is it then? I will pray with the spirit, and I will pray with the understand-*

ing also: I will sing with the spirit, and I will sing with the understanding also." I Corinthians 14:18, *"I thank my God, I speak with tongues more than ye all."*

Now, there are times when you can pray in tongues just because you want to. The Bible does not say, "Thou must be in thy church and on thy knees and on thy face before thou canst pray and God will hear thee." You can pray anywhere, anytime. We have records of Jesus praying on mountain tops, praying on the side of a hill, praying standing up, praying sitting down, with his eyes open and with his eyes closed, looking up and looking down.

There are times when the spirit of intercession will come upon you and it will be like a flood. It will seem as though you cannot stop it. That is the spirit of intercession. It is actually the Spirit of God within you making intercession on behalf of people. At the same time you can pray in other tongues yourself and the Spirit of God will interject your spirit with the right words to say so you will pray according to the will of God. But other times God will call you to intercession. He may wake you up in the middle of the night as He has done with me. Do not turn Him down. Get up and enter into one of the greatest thrills of life — interceding with the Holy Ghost!

CHAPTER VII
INTERCEDING AGAINST THE POWERS OF DARKNESS

Let us read again in Ephesians 6:10-18, *"Finally, my brethren, be strong in the Lord, and in the power of his might. Put on the whole armour of God, that you may be able to stand against the wiles of the devil. For we wrestle not against flesh and blood, but* (we wrestle) *against principalities, against powers, against the rulers of the darkness of this world, against spiritual wickedness in high places* (or against wicked spirits in heavenly places). *Wherefore take unto you the whole armour of God, that ye may be able to withstand in the evil day, and having done all, to stand. Stand therefore, having your loins girt about with truth, and having on the breastplate of righteousness; And your feet shod with the preparation of the gospel of peace: Above all, taking the shield of faith, wherewith ye shall be able to quench all the fiery darts of the wicked. And take the helmet of salvation, and the sword of the Spirit, which is the word of God: praying always with all prayer and supplication in the Spirit, and watching thereunto with all perseverance and supplication for all saints."*

Many people read these verses concerning the armor of God and they see the need to take unto them the whole armor of God and to have His armor upon them, but what is the armor for? In verses 17 and 18, *"And take the helmet of salvation, and the sword of the Spirit, which is the word of God: Praying..."* This armor has been given to wear in prayer. This is prayer armor, combat armor. You do not wear armor to ice cream socials, you wear armor to do combat — warfare.

Now, whether you realize it or not you are involved in a spiritual war. There is warfare going on around you and warfare being made against you all the time. It is amazing how many people live their entire lives ignorant of this fact. They live in such a way that this warfare causes things to happen in their lives and their attitude is, "That is the way the old ball bounces, the way the cookie crumbles. That is just fate, it just happened by chance." I want you to know that there is nothing that happens by chance. Everything happens by design or plan — your's, God's or Satan's.

Christian people like to say, "Well, God is in control." They like to say that particularly when they look around and see all the wickedness going on and somebody will say, "Isn't it good to know that God is in control?" To an extent God is in control. But there are a lot of things that go on that God is not in favor of one way or the other. Many Christians get upset when people say, "If God is in control, then He is sure doing a lousy job." Those people are talking from a standpoint of looking at what is going on in the earth. The point is that there are a lot of things that God is not in control of. We need to realize that. There are a lot of things that go on in the earth that God did not have anything to do with.

In a recent article I read that in the United States alone in one year there are over 1.5 million abortions. God is not in favor of that. God says that is murder. It is no different in the eyes of God just because that little fellow was conceived six weeks ago than if someone took the child when he was six years old and shot him with a gun. It is not different in the eyes of God. But just because God does not like it does not mean that it is going to be stopped. If you have made a mistake concerning abortion and did not know better, I want you to know right now that I am not condemning you and neither is God. There are a lot of things that go on in your life, in your personal life that God does not like and they will still go on. God sent Jesus to help us.

Daniel 10:1, *"In the third year of Cyrus king of Persia a thing was revealed unto Daniel, whose name was Belteshazzar; and the thing was true, but the time appointed was long: and he understood the thing, and had understanding of the vision. In those days I Daniel was mourning three full weeks. I ate no pleasant bread, neither came flesh or wine in my mouth, neither did I anoint myself at all, till three whole weeks were fulfilled. And in the four and twentieth day of the first month, as I was by the side of the great river, which is Hiddekel; Then I lifted up mine eyes, and looked and behold, a certain man clothed in linen..."* Daniel is by a river. He has been praying and fasting. He has been on a partial fast. He has been eating just enough to sustain himself. At the end of three weeks while he is praying, God reveals some things to him through a man that he describes as being, *"...clothed in linen, whose loins were girded with fine gold of Uphaz: His body also was like the beryl, and his face as the appearance of lightning, and his eyes as lamps of fire, and his arms and his feet like in colour to polished brass, and the voice of his words like the voice of a multitude."* Not the type of man that you would see on the street and just give a passing glance.

"And I Daniel alone saw the vision: for the men that were with me saw not the vision; but a great quaking fell upon them, so that they fled to hide themselves." The others could not see him. Only Daniel could see him, but they knew something was happening and they went and hid themselves. *"Therefore I was left alone, and saw this great vision, and there remained no strength in me: for*

my comeliness or vigor was turned in me into corruption, and I retained no strength. Yet heard I the voice of his words: and when I heard the voice of his words, then was I in a deep sleep on my face, and my face toward the ground. And, behold, an hand touched me, which set me upon my knees and upon the palms of my hands." Daniel was lying flat on his face and this being touched him and picked him up to where he was able to get up on his hands and knees. *"And he said unto me, O Daniel, a man greatly beloved, understand the words that I speak unto thee, and stand upright: for unto thee am I now sent. And when he had spoken this word unto me, I stood trembling. Then said he unto me, Fear not, Daniel: for from the first day that thou didst set thine heart to understand, and to chasten thyself before thy God, thy words were heard,* (When were his words heard in heaven? The first day.) *and I am come for thy words."*

What caused the angel to come? Daniel's words, his words drew God's response which was to send this angel. When were the words heard? The first day.

"But the prince of the kingdom of Persia withstood me one and twenty days: (three weeks) *but, lo, Michael, one of the chief princes, came to help me; and I remained there with the kings of Persia. Now I am come to make thee understand what shall befall thy people in the latter days: for yet the vision is for many days."*

Daniel chastened himself and fasted for twenty-one days. The **first day** he prayed God dispatched this angel to bring him the answer. On his way from heaven to Daniel he had to pass through another spiritual kingdom.

THREE HEAVENS

Now the Bible talks about three different kinds of heavens. The first heaven is the heaven you can see with your physical eyes —the sky, the atmosphere that encircles our planet. The second heaven is the stars and the planets beyond our own atmosphere and the third heaven is where God lives. In Ephesians we read that we wrestle against wicked spirits in heavenly places. This angel came to Daniel from heaven, where God lives, but there was something that stopped him. He said the prince of Persia withstood him. Does he mean that the physical man, the prince of Persia stopped him? By no means. There is not a man alive who can stand up to an angel of God who desires to go his own way. Angels are messengers that do what God tells them. They do not make decisions for themselves about what God tells them. Angels do what they are told, and if God says go down and tell Daniel, they go down and tell Daniel.

Verse 13, *"But the prince of the kingdom of Persia withstood me one and twenty days; but, lo, Michael, one of the chief princes, came to help me ..."* This angel had to get reinforcements — Michael, the archangel, had to come down and do spiritual battle. They were not fighting with a flesh and blood man, but against the wicked spirit that ruled a spiritual kingdom above the natural kingdom. Over a city or a nation where you have earthly rulers Satan will set up a spiritual kingdom above that physical kingdom, and through the spiritual kingdom he will try to rule the natural kingdom. The angel was sent to bring the message, but he could not get through. He did not have enough power on his own to fight his way through that spiritual kingdom. Therefore, Michael, the war angel, came down and fought with the prince of Persia and got the angel through to Daniel.

Verse 20, *"...Knowest thou wherefore I come unto thee? and now will I return to fight with the prince of Persia ..."* When he went back, then he would have to fight with him again. The angel continued and said, *"...and when I am gone forth, lo, the prince of Grecia shall come."* History tells us that Grecia replaced Persia as a world ruler. There was such combat in that spiritual realm between Michael and this angel and the prince of Persia that they were going to absolutely destroy that spiritual kingdom. When they destroyed it, the physical kingdom would also collapse and a new kingdom would come in named Grecia. Satan will try to set up these spiritual kingdoms and they must be torn down.

Ezekiel 28:1, *"The word of the Lord came again unto me, saying, Son of man, say unto the prince of Tyrus, Thus saith the Lord God; Because thine heart is lifted up, and because thou hast said I am a God, I sit in the seat of God, in the midst of the seas; yet thou art a man ..."*

Now who is he talking to? The prince of Tyrus. What is he? He is a man who thinks he is God. *"...thou art a man, and not god."* Verse 11, *"Moreover the word of the Lord came unto me, saying, Son of man, take up a lamentation upon the king of Tyrus,* (who was the first one spoken to? — the prince of Tyrus) *and say unto him, Thus saith the Lord God; thou sealest up the sum, full of wisdom, and perfect in beauty. Thou hast been in Eden the garden of God; every precious stone was thy covering, the sardius, topaz and the diamond, the beryl, the onyx, and the jasper, the sapphire, the emerald and the carbuncle, and gold: the workmanship of thy tabrets and of thy pipes was prepared in thee in the day that thou wast created. Thou are the anointed cherub that covereth; and I have set thee so: Thou wast upon the holy mountain of God; thou hast walked up and down in the midst of the stones of fire. Thou wast perfect in thy ways from the day that thou wast created, till iniquity was found in thee.*

Who is he talking to here? He is talking to Satan. The first time he talked to the prince of Tyrus. The second time he talked to the king of Tyrus. Satan himself had set up a reign over the prince of Tyrus. The prince of Tyrus called himself God because he was influenced by the spiritual being — Satan himself — who has been trying to become like God since iniquity was found in him.

Verse 17, *"Thine heart was lifted up because of thy beauty, thou hast corrupted thy wisdom by reason of thy brightness: I will cast thee to the ground, I will lay thee before kings, that they may behold thee. Thou hast defiled thy sanctuaries by the multitude of thine iniquities, by the iniquity of thy traffick; therefore will I bring forth a fire from the midst of thee, it shall devour thee, and I will bring thee to ashes upon the earth in the sight of all them that behold thee. All they that know thee among the people shall be astonished at thee: thou shalt be a terror and never shalt thou be any more."*

There are spiritual kingdoms, wicked spirits in heavenly places that influence nations and cities and those things are dealt with through intercessory prayer. They are handled by people praying and interceding.

II Corinthians 4:4 says that Satan is the god of this world and he blinds the minds of them that believe not. I John 5:19, *"And we know that we are of God, and the whole world lieth in wickedness."* The literal Greek text says, "And the whole world lies in the embrace of the evil one." People who have not made Jesus the Lord of their life, who have not accepted Him as their Lord and their Saviour, lie in the embrace of Satan. I know they do not do it on purpose, but it still happens.

Colossians 1:12, *"Giving thanks unto the Father, which hath made us meet to be partakers of the inheritance of the saints in light: who hath delivered us from the power of darkness ..."* What have we been delivered from? From the power of darkness. The word "power" is better translated authority. We have been delivered from the authority of darkness and we have been translated into the kingdom of God's dear Son. When you made Jesus the Lord of your life, God took you out of the kingdom of darkness and translated you into the kingdom of light. He has moved you from one kingdom to the other. There are multitudes of people who are living in the kingdom of darkness; they lay in the embrace of Satan, whose effects are upon them.

Ephesians 6:10, *"Finally my brethren, be strong in the Lord, and in the power of his might. Put on the whole armour of God ..."* Why do you put on the armor of God? So that you may pray. In verse 18, *"...with all* (kinds of) *prayer and supplication in the Spirit..."*, or as the Goodsby translation says, *"pray with every kind of prayer and entreaty and pray in the spirit at every opportunity."*

The armor that God has given you is to use in spiritual combat against the wicked spirits that control men's lives around you. In Ephesians 6:12 it tells us that we wrestle against these spiritual beings. The way Satan is controlled in the earth today is through the body of Christ. The book of Hebrews says that Jesus is resting until we make His enemies His footstool. We are the ones who do the wrestling. We wrestle against these principalities and powers, against the rulers of the darkness of this world, against wicked spirits in high or heavenly places. When we go into this combat, we are to put on the whole armor of God. You get to wear the whole armor of God and remember, this is prayer armor.

Men are and can be influenced by spiritual beings. Romans 8:14 says that we are led by the spirit of God. Ephesians 2:1-3 says that before we became Christians we were children of disobedience led by the spirit of disobedience.

Oftentimes people will pray for somebody or something and, as I have said previously in this book, they will take the rules that govern the prayer of petition and try to make those rules work in the area of intercession. You cannot do that anymore than you can take football rules and play baseball with them. A lot of Christians experience this — they see a need in someone's life or they begin praying for someone and they say to themselves, "Jesus said whatsoever things you desire when you pray, believe you receive them and you shall have them. Father, I believe my uncle is saved." Years go by and someone else says, "I do not understand why your uncle has not gotten saved," and they say, "Bless God, I prayed the prayer of faith, he is saved." You cannot do that. That is like going to a football game to see people hit home runs. For all you ladies reading this, they do not hit home runs in football.

It is so vital that you understand this about intercessory prayer. You cannot do that even for people who are born again, who are living contrary to God's ways. You cannot force God's blessing upon them, nor can you make them obedient to God's Word. You cannot just walk up and say, "Charles, I want you to agree with me that my uncle is going to get saved." I will agree with you, I will pray with you, but I am going to pray first of all that laborers come into his path. I am going to bind the devil in his life. But if that old boy is walking contrary to God — God will set him free again. What is going to make the difference is perseverance in prayer.

Ephesians 6:18, *"Praying always with all prayer and supplication in the Spirit, and watching thereunto with all perseverance and supplication for all the saints."* There are certain people whom I can pray the prayer of faith for. I mean a simple prayer of petition. All prayers are prayers of faith or you are better off not praying. But there are certain people I can pray this simple prayer of petition for. I can pray it for myself. "Father, in the name of Jesus I am asking you to heal me. I believe I receive my healing now." I can pray for my wife, I can pray for my children, I can pray it for certain baby Christians. James chapter five gives me the right to do that.

It says, that if there is any sick among you, let him call for the elders of the church who will come and anoint him with oil and the prayer of faith shall save the sick and the Lord shall raise him up.

I can pray the prayer of faith for certain baby Christians, but I cannot stand on the sidewalk and point at people who come by and say, "Father, I believe that one is saved, etc." There are people who think like that. What should you do? You begin to intercede on their behalf, make yourself sensitive to their needs, begin to pray for them and intercede for them and begin to reach out to God for them. You do spiritual combat on their behalf.

A lot of people do not know they are living in darkness. They think they are living in the light. They think what they are doing is right. They think where they are going is the right way to go. You must stand up and fight for them. You must fight the fight of faith. You must use the weapons of your warfare, which are not carnal but mighty through God, for the pulling down of the strongholds (II Corinthians 10:3-5) that Satan builds up over peoples' lives, and sometimes it takes more than fifteen minutes. Sometimes you will have to travail for them. Take their weaknesses upon you and pray and intercede for them, and cry out to God on their behalf, and do spiritual combat for them. You get the devil off their backs and you keep him off until they get sensitive enough to turn to the light and get born again. But this has been so hard for people to understand because many of them — when they look in this area — they do not want to take the time.

NOT JUST WHEN YOU FEEL LIKE IT

Praying for the lost and interceding against the powers of darkness are not things you do just any time you feel like it. You pray when you don't feel like it. You pray because they need help. I believe in the prayer of faith; I believe in the prayer of petition; I live by them. John 16:23, Mark 11:24, Matthew 21:22 — I believe in those scriptures and I pray them for myself and my family. Sometimes I can pray them for others, but not all the time. Sometimes I must pray the prayer of intercession.

I know, if I do not pray, nothing is going to happen. If you want to see people get saved, if you want to see people get healed, if you want to see people turn their lives around, then you must spend time in prayer. You break the power of the devil and give place to God's power through prayer. Prayer makes things happen and come to pass.

Oftentimes while in prayer, Christians will feel in their own spirits as though they are lost. What is sad is that many of them do not know what is happening. They think maybe they really are not saved. Do you know what it really is? It is the spirit of intercession that has come upon their spirit to pray for some lost person whom God is trying to reach, and they are feeling in their spirit what that other person is feeling in his spirit — the sensation of being lost. When that happens, if you will pray and pray and pray until that feeling lifts from you, you will soon see somebody get born again.

God forgive us for being so spiritually illiterate. We have so much to learn in these areas.

THE LOST ART

Intercession is the single greatest lost art in the church today. We have become masters at everything except intercession. That is why we have laws trying to be passed in Congress which are absolutely absurd, that is why we have people in political offices who are ding-a-lings, that is why there is so much wickedness loose in the earth today. All of this is happening, and so many members of the body of Christ are standing around saying, "I wish Jesus would come today." I do not have time for that. People are dying and going to hell and it is intercession that breaks the power of the devil. We need people who will put on the whole armor of God to fight and wrestle with those demonic spirits, so those things can be cast out of people's lives. We need people who are willing to pray so God can move in people's lives and bring the light to them. The devil has them blinded. Blind men cannot see the light. We must get the blindness off them. The way it is done is by taking the name of Jesus and praying for hours, or weeks if need be, until it breaks Satan's power.

A lot of people experience failure in their lives, and the members of their family do not come into the kingdom of God because there is no intercession.

The Bible says in Ephesians 2 that I am a member of the household of God, I am a citizen of heaven. I can demand my heavenly rights for myself and to a certain extent I can demand your heavenly rights for you, but I cannot make you take them. I can demand your national right as a citizen of the United States to be able to vote, but I cannot make you go and vote. I can get you the right to vote but you must do it for yourself. I can demand your right to be healed, but you must receive it. For myself I can demand my own rights and say, "Devil, get out of my affairs in the name of Jesus and get out now!" But when you find someone walking contrary to the laws of God and living in sin, he has opened himself up to the devil. Satan can plead his case against him as well as you can plead your case for him. Satan can say, "I know this man is wrong and that gives me the right to be in his life and influence him." If that is the case, then you must take the name of Jesus and the sword of the spirit and make it so uncomfortable for Satan that he does not want to stay around there.

THE SPIRIT OF INTERCESSION

Now, there are times after you become involved in intercession when the spirit of intercession will come upon you when you are at work or while you are driving your car or in the strangest places. One time I was in a restaurant and preparing to order when the spirit of intercession came upon me and I said to the waitress, "I'll be back." She said, "Is there something wrong?" I said, "There is nothing wrong." On the inside of me I felt as though I was going to explode! I went back to my motel room so I could pray. The Holy Ghost in me was wanting me to pray. I do not know how many hours I prayed. When you get over into that realm with God you get like the Lord Jesus Christ in the fourth chapter of John with the woman at the well of Samaria. Men came to Him and said, "Aren't you hungry?" He said, "I have food to eat that you do not even know of. My meat is to do the will of my Father." Your flesh lies down and shuts up when you step over into the spirit realm like that.

You see it is through intercession that you get the devil off your back. You wrestle against those spiritual powers and get them out of your life. People have problems in their lives and they do not understand why and they say, "I have been using my confession." Have you been interceding? Have you been taking your weapons that God has given you and launching an attack against those demonic spirits? Have you been fighting against them as much as they have been fighting against you? You can take your confession of faith and hit the devil smooth in the face and knock him flat. Sometimes though he will just jump right back up. So take the name of Jesus and pray in the spirit and go after him.

This is how you win others to Jesus — through intercession. It is not through neat little programs, it is through intercession. It is itercession that makes the programs work. Intercession greases the wheels of the evangelism wagon of God.

Romans 12:11, *"Not slothful in business; fervent in spirit..."* The word fervent means white-hot or to boil. It also means to be earnest. There needs to be fervency in our spirits. We need to get hot on the inside, boiling on the inside and be earnest in our prayers. Sometimes you must stand up and fight for something that is dear to you.

Ephesians 6 says, *"...and having done all, to stand. Stand therefore ..."* The literal Greek text says, "stand your ground". You need to fight for your families, relatives, cities, jobs, businesses, neighborhoods. Do not let the devil have them.

We need to learn to be sensitive to these urges to pray. It may happen at any time. You may wake up in the middle of the night. If you make yourself sensitive, eventually you will find yourself praying all day long.

CHAPTER VIII
INTERCEDING FOR THE SAINTS

Ephesians 6:18, *"Praying always with all prayer and supplication in the spirit,* (Goodsby translation — use every kind of prayer and entreaty and pray in the Spirit at very opportunity) *and watching thereunto with all perseverance and supplication for all the saints."*

Who are you watching for? All the saints. We are going to talk now about praying for the saints. God has more saints than just those who are in heaven who have been designated Saint so and so. In the mind of God, every born-again person is a saint.

He said, *"...watching thereunto with all perseverance and supplication for all the saints."* Why do we watch in perseverance for the saints? Because we are members one of another. I Corinthians 12 beginning in verse 12, Paul begins to talk about the similarity between the physical human body and the body of Christ. In verse 26, *"And whether one member* (one member of what? one member of the body) *suffer, all the members suffer with it..."* Isn't that true? There are parts of your body that seem to be more important than other parts. You may think that part of your body is unimportant until something happens to it. Paul, by the direction of the Holy Spirit, is showing us the way it should be and must be in the body of Christ. When one member suffers, we should all suffer.

"Charles, does that mean if one of us gets sick we are all supposed to get sick?" No. "Does that mean if one of us goes broke we are all supposed to go broke?" What do you think? No, that is not what he is saying.

Romans 15:1, *"We then that are strong ought to*

bear the infirmities of the weak, and not to please ourselves." Galatians 6:2, *"Bear ye one another's burdens, and so fulfil the law of Christ."* Now the word "bear" in those two verses literally means "to lift with the idea of removing." He said that the strong are to lift with the idea of removing, not just lift so they can manage and then give it back to them.

Do you see the difference? God plans on your doing something with your prayer life and affecting the well-being of other people.

BELIEVERS WHO BELIEVE WRONG

He said, lift with the idea of removing the infirmities of the weak. Now the word "infirmities" in Romans 15 and Galatians 6 means "a scruple of conscience, or something that is wrong in a person's belief."

Have you ever known anyone who had something wrong in their believing? Some people are wrong in their believing in the area of healing. They believe that God wants them sick. For example, I meet a person, and I talk to them, and I discover that there is something wrong in their believing. I can either begin to pray and intercede on their behalf, with the purpose of lifting that off them to remove it so they will no longer be wrong in their believing, or I can say, "What a dummy they are, how stupid they are." Remember, if God could get to you, He can get to anybody. We tend to magnify things and blow them out of proportion when we see them in others. When you look at things from God's vantage point, the problems in our lives are not very big. God does not take the attitude that it is not worth His time, because He is interested in us, and He cares about us.

Do you know how the body of Christ is going to be perfected? Through intercessory prayer. The body of Christ is going to be perfected through intercessory prayer. What did the apostle Paul do when he heard of something wrong in the church? He began to pray and intercede for them.

WEIGHED DOWN

Hebrews 12:1,2 shows us that Christian people get weighed down and they faint. Have you ever seen a Christian faint in their faith and their walk with God? It happens. A good percentage of the time, that could be avoided by the Christians around im interceding. I know at times it is much easier just to let them go. I have had that temptation and, with some people, no matter how much you pray for them, they are still going to fall away. But, that is still a very small percentage. Some Christians get weighed down in unbelief.

Galatians 4:19, *"My little children, of whom I travail in birth again until Christ be formed in you."* Paul wrote this to the Galatians, people whom he had been responsible for bringing into the family of God. A church that God had commissioned him and anointed him to raise up. He heard about the problems that they were having in what they were believing. They wanted to go back to live under the law. He said, *"I will travail in birth again."* That shows that he travailed in birth once before. When did he travail in birth before? When they were first born again. Paul did not have the attitude, "They are saved, they are filled with the Holy Ghost, if they have anything, they will make it." He began to intercede on their behalf. He did not just pray a general prayer. He said, *"My little children, of whom I travail in birth again until Christ be formed in you."* He had a desired purpose and an end result that he was moving towards. He said that he was going to travail in birth until Christ was formed in them or, "I am going to do this until I see it happen."

Oftentimes, not only do the people who are being prayed for get discouraged, but also the person who is doing the praying. You must be willing to invest some time and some effort.

INVESTING IN PEOPLE

You are not going to get something for nothing. You are going to have to be willing to invest something in what you are doing — time, effort and diligence.

That is the reason why so many marriages fail, because they have a 50-50 attitude. Marriage is not 50-50, but 100-100. It is a commitment — a 100% commitment.

He said that he was going to travail again until Christ was formed in them. If we will begin to pray and intercede for Christians, then a lot of weird things that people do will change. Griping about it, complaining about it, hollering about it, talking about it, making fun of it and pointing it out will not make things better. They will remain the same. They will not change.

The only way people are going to change is through intercession.

INABILITY TO PRODUCE

Romans 8:22, *"For we know that the whole creation groaneth and travaileth in pain together until now. And not only they, but ourselves also, which have the first fruits of the Spirit ..."* Do you think God is producing everything in your life that He can produce? Would you say that he is producing the first fruits? Then he must be talking about us.

"And not only they, but ourselves also, which have the first fruits of the Spirit, even we ourselves groan within ourselves, waiting for the adoption, to wit, the redemption of our body. For we are saved by hope: but hope that is seen is not hope: for what a man seeth, why doth he yet hope for? But if we hope for that we see not, then do we with patience wait for it."

If there is one single ingredient that you must have in praying for the saints, it is patience, or consistency. It is the consistent, continual, effectual prayer of the righteous man that avails much. (James 5:16).

We are talking about praying for people. Have you ever prayed for yourself more than once? Sure you have. If you need to be prayed for more than once, what makes you think that you do not need to pray for me more than once? Verse 26, *"Likewise the Spirit also helpeth our infirmities..."* The word "infirmities" here means "helps our want of strength, our weaknesses, or inability to produce results."

How many times I have looked at my life and seen things I needed and could not get it to produce. I could not get it to come to pass. I could see it, I knew it was God's will for me to have it, I knew what God wanted me to do with it when I got it, but I could not get it to come to pass. Have you ever experienced that? Inability to produce the result. How many times I have had people come to me and say, "Charles, I do not understand it, I prayed and it just does not seem to come to pass." *"Likewise the Spirit also helpeth our infirmities: for we know not what we should pray for as we ought: but the Spirit itself maketh intercession..."* What did Ephesians 6 say?

Praying always in the Spirit for all the saints. *"...but the Spirit itself maketh intercession for us with groanings which cannot be uttered. And he that searcheth the hearts knoweth what is the mind of the Spirit, because he maketh intercession for the saints according to the will of God."*

I John 5:14-15 tells us that if we pray according to God's will He hears us. We know that if He hears us then we have the petitions we desired of Him.

So, the pivot point in prayer is to get God to hear you. How do you get God to hear you? You must pray according to His will. The Bible says that the spirit of God in us will make intercession for us according to the will of God.

TRAVAILING IN BIRTH

Now, let us back up a minute — did you notice a repetition of several words in these verses? Verse 22, *"...creation groaneth and travaileth ..."* Verse 23, *"And not only they, but ourselves also ..."* Verse 26, *"...But the spirit itself maketh intercession for us with groanings which cannot be uttered."*

Have you ever seen a woman give birth to a child? She groans, she travails in birth until the child is born.

Isaiah 66:8, *"Who hath heard such a thing? who hath seen such things? Shall the earth be made to bring forth in one day? or shall a nation be born at once? for as soon as Zion travailed, she brought forth her children."* Hebrews 12:18-23 reveals to us that we are Zion — the church is Zion. What did he say happens when Zion travailed? She brings forth her children.

Do you want to see people born again in your church? Then start praying and interceding and travailing and crying out to God until those things are brought forth and those people are born again into the kingdom of God. Now some people just read the Bible and get saved. Nobody had to travail for them. And there are some people in the body of Christ that you do not have to travail in birth for them until Christ is formed in them. They take it upon themselves to grow. Some people, but not everybody. Not everybody is like that.

Not all babies are the same. Some of them you have to do more for. Some children need more attention than other children. The same thing is true spiritually. Some people get saved and filled with the Holy Spirit and somebody needs to travail for them again till Christ is formed in them.

Let us look again at verses 26 and 27, *"Likewise the Spirit also helpeth our infirmities..."* The word "helpeth" in the Greek text is actually three Greek words that read like this. "For the Spirit also takes hold together with us against," or "the Spirit takes hold together with us against our inabilities to produce fruit." He takes hold together with us against these inabilities, these weaknesses, whatever they may be — spiritually, physically, financially, mentally or socially. He does it with you. He does not do it for you. He said, *"Likewise the Spirit also takes hold together with us against our inabilities to produce results. For we know not what we should pray for as we ought but the Spirit himself makes intercession for us with groanings that cannot be uttered."*

P.C. Nelson, the great Greek Bible scholar, said those verses should go on and say, "with groanings that cannot be uttered in articulate speech." He is talking about a travailing in your spirit, a groaning that comes up in your heart that escapes your lips. Paul compared it to travailing in birth. If you have ever watched a woman give birth to a child you know that groaning comes from down in her innermost being. What happens when that groaning ceases? A life is born. The same thing is true in the spiritual realm. God uses the natural to explain the spiritual.

I am talking about praying for the saints till Christ is formed in them.

COMMITTED

You need to pray for me. I need to pray for you. We are not perfect, and we are not going to get that way until we start praying for one another.

I am not talking about, "Lord, today bless this one, bless that one, Amen." You are wasting your time and playing spiritual games. I am talking about the power that can change nations. I am talking about the power that can change the course of history.

If you will study church history, you will find men and women who laid on their faces before God and cried out in the spirit of God and moaned until revival broke out in their churches or cities. You have got to work at this. It is something that you must allow God to teach you. I can give you examples, but you must work into it.

So many times when people pray, they do so for fifteen minutes watching their clock. They do not put themselves into it. They are not committed to it. They have not dedicated themselves. Many people want to experience spiritual things but they do not want to be available to experience it. Many people want to see the saints grow, but they are not willing to pray for them. Many people want to see their church grow, but are not willing to pray.

It is one thing to have a lot of decisions, but it is another thing to have a lot of births. There are people who follow Jesus, but they never make Jesus the Lord of their lives, therefore they are not born again. The only way you are going to get them born again is if somebody intercedes for them.

If you want to see your city turned on to Jesus, it will require laying down your life to travail until people get born again. It is not going to happen by great programs. It is not going to happen because of good teachers.

EXAMPLES IN CHARLES FINNEY'S LIFE

Charles Finney had a man who worked for him, called Father Nash. Father Nash would go to a town where Brother Finney was going to be preaching, about three days ahead of Brother Finney. He would lock himself in a boarding house, and for three days and three nights he would fast and pray. Now, when Brother Finney would do a meeting, he would stay for at least six months. Many times he would stay for a year. He would preach every night except Saturday and Monday for six months or a year. He had such a tremendous revival in Rochester, New York, that they shut down all the bars and poured all the whiskey in the streets. There was a circus that came to town while he was doing the meeting, and only two people went. They shut the circus down and moved on to another town. It is not that Brother Finney was preaching against the circus, because he did not. Those attending were so enthralled with spiritual things and with people getting born again, that they did not have time for the circus.

One time, Brother Finney came to a town and went to see Father Nash. When he went to the boarding house, a woman stopped him and said, "Are you Mr. Finney? Do you know that man up there that they call Father Nash? Is there something wrong with him? Ever since he got here, he has been in his room moaning and groaning. He never comes down to eat and if I wake up in the middle of the night I can hear him in there moaning. I walked into his room the other day. I thought maybe he was sick and dying, so I opened up his door and there he was on the floor groaning and crying out to God." Finney said, "There is nothing wrong. He is travailing in the spirit." The power of God would fall on those towns so strong they were overwhelmed by it.

Many people think they have to wait for the spirit of intercession to come upon them. Sometimes the spirit of intercession will come upon you, but sometimes you must get up and begin to pray. Smith Wigglesworth said, "if the Spirit is not moving, move the Spirit."

During a particular meeting, Mr. Finney had a Monday off. There was a woman who attended the meeting whose husband was a doctor. He was a very prominent man, a very successful man, and a professed atheist. This woman was trying so hard to get him saved and the harder she tried, the harder he got. She asked Brother Finney over to eat one day, a set up, you see. Mr. Finney did not know this until he got there. She also invited her husband's brother who was an old farmer. Her husband looked down on this brother because he was not educated as he was, also he was not as prosperous and successful, but his brother was a born-again Christian. They had a magnificent house and the servants prepared a great meal. They all came in to eat and the little woman was so anxious. Brother Finney stood up to pray for the meal and after he said about two sentences, he had a check in his spirit. He stopped and turned to the brother (the farmer) and said, "I feel in my heart that God wants you to pray over the food."

So the farmer began to pray and uttered about two or three words when he grabbed his stomach and ran upstairs. The doctor ran into his study and got his medical bag and followed him. Brother Finney ran up the stairs with the doctor and when they opened the bedroom door, the man was kneeling beside the bed crying out from inside his spirit. The doctor said, "I wonder what is wrong with him?" Brother Finney said, "There is nothing wrong with him. He is just travailing in the spirit for some poor, lost, hellbound sinner. Probably you." The doctor turned around and slammed the door behind himself as he went down the stairs. He locked himself in the library and would not let anyone in.

Brother Finney knelt down next to the farmer and started praying with him. They prayed together for about thirty or forty-five minutes until a note of victory came into their hearts. They then began to laugh and thank the Lord. Soon they both got up and went downstairs. The brother sat down at the table. The woman said to Mr. Finney, "Well, the meal is ruined, and my husband is in the library, and he will never speak to me. This whole thing has turned out wrong." Brother Finney said, "Where is your husband?" She showed him where the library was. Brother Finney knocked on the door and said, "This is Brother Finney and I desire to speak with you." The man opened the door and Brother Finney said, "It is alright now. Your brother has prayed and travailed in the spirit and you are not going to have to go to hell. He has saved you from the jaws of death. He has prayed you through. Do not worry about it, everything is alright. Your brother is fine and you are not going to have to go to hell." As he turned to walk away, the doctor fell to the floor and made Jesus the Lord of his life. He went on to be a great soldier in the kingdom, a great man in that community.

Do you want to see things like that? Do you want to see people get born into the kingdom of God? Then you are going to have to birth them. You have to give of yourself on their behalf. Do you want to see Christians change and get things out of their believing that are wrong? Then you must be willing to pray for them, intercede for them, travail in the spirit for them. Get God to help you and teach you in these things.

Sometimes baby Christians need intercessors to help them walk. They need somebody to help them, pick them up and carry them. Do you know who those somebodies are? You and me, because we know these things and when you know them you become responsible for them.

CHAPTER IX
INTERCEDING
FOR THE NATION

There are different kinds of prayer. There is the prayer of petition. There is the prayer of intercession. There is praying in the spirit. There is the prayer of agreement. There is united prayer. There is the prayer of thanksgiving. There are many different kinds of prayer. Goodsby said that we should use every kind of prayer and entreaty and pray in the spirit at every opportunity.

I Timothy 2:1, *"I exhort therefore, that, first of all, supplications, prayers, intercession, and giving of thanks be made for all men; For kings and for all that are in authority; that we may lead a quiet and peaceable life in all godliness and honesty. For this is good and acceptable in the sight of God our Saviour; Who will have all men to be saved, and to come into the knowledge of the truth. For there is one God, and one mediator between God and men, the man Christ Jesus. Who gave himself a ransom for all, to be testified in due time."*

I want us to talk about interceding for our nation. Let us read this verse again — *"I exhort therefore, that first of all, supplications, prayers, intercessions, and giving of thanks be made for all men."* "Charles, am I supposed to pray for everybody, every day?" No. Of course we can say, "Father, save China, thank you." You will cover a big piece of the world right there. Somehow, I do not think that is what Paul had in mind in this verse of scripture. In verse two he tells us to pray for kings, or presidents, or prime ministers and for all who are in authority.

EFFECTING OUR NATION

We can have a positive effect on the course of our lems nation through intercessory prayer. A lot of probthat are happening in our country today are the result of wicked, ungodly men. They are also the result of non-praying Christians. Most of us are very critical of the job that our politicians do. But if they were as slothful about their jobs as Christians have been about praying for them, they would not even be showing up for work.

We can have a tremendous effect on the course of our nation through intercessory prayer. "Charles, what good does it do for us to pray if the people who are in authority are not even Christians. Can we have any effect?" Yes, we have a tremendous effect. Read with me — *"I exhort therefore, that first of all supplications, prayers, intercessions, and giving of thanks be made for all men; For kings and for all that are in authority..."* I think it is interesting that he used the word "exhort" when it comes to interceding for those in authority. I have found that in my life, when it comes to interceding for those who are in authority, be it political, economic or social, that it is very easy to become discouraged.

I want to exhort you to pray and intercede. We can have an effect upon the course of this country. He said, *"I exhort therefore, that first of all..."* When it comes to things like this, we need to get our priorities in line. Christians need to become politically involved. We need to do more than just sit around and gripe. I must also caution you in this area. We can become as politically involved as we want, but the only way we are going to have effective power is if we are oiling our involvement with intercession.

Intercession is the power of the church. Let us be careful that we do not put our trust in any man other than Jesus Christ. Psalm 118 says that it is better to trust in the Lord than it is to trust in princes or people who are in authority.

PEACEFUL AND QUIET LIVES

We need to put our confidence in the things that are eternal. We are to pray for all who are in authority. Why? So that we may lead a quiet and a peaceable life in all godliness and honesty. If you are believing in some political party to produce peace and quietness in your life, you are in for a real surprise. *"Pray, first of all, for kings and all that are in authority.* (Why?) *So that we may lead a quiet and peaceable life in all godliness and honesty. For this is good and acceptable in the sight of God our Saviour; Who will have all men to be saved and come into the knowledge of the truth."* What does verse four have to do with verses two and three? What does salvation have to do with us leading a quiet and peaceable life? For one reason, when there are wars and rumors of wars the Gospel is not going to spread. The devil would like nothing better than to get the United States in a panic and get us all worried and frightened, and shut down. Why? Because 90% of the missionaries in the foreign field come from the United States of America. We are the seed bed of evangelism for the world.

He said, *"For this is good and acceptable in the sight of God our Saviour who would have all men to be saved and come into the knowledge of the truth."* Our trust cannot be in men. We need to put first things first. The first thing is prayer and intercession and the giving of thanks on behalf of kings and all who are in authority.

ABRAHAM IN ACTION

In Genesis 18 God comes down and visits Abraham on the plains of Mamre. Abraham is sitting outside of his tent. God appears with two angels. They are on their way to Sodom and Gomorrah.

Genesis 18:16, *"And the men rose up from thence, and looked towards Sodom: and Abraham went with them to bring them on the way. And the Lord said, Shall I hide from Abraham that thing which I do; Seeing that Abraham shall become a great and mighty nation, and all the nations of the earth shall be blessed in him? For I know him that he will command his children and his household after him, and they shall keep the way of the Lord, to do justice and judgment; that the Lord may bring upon Abraham that which he has spoken of him. And the Lord said, because the cry of Sodom and Gomorrah is great and because their sin is very grevious; I will go down now and see whether they have done all together according to the cry of it, which is come unto me; and if not, I will know. And the men turned their faces from thence, and went toward Sodom: but Abraham stood yet before the Lord."*

We have the Father and two angels. They have come to Abraham while on their way to Sodom and Gomorrah. He tells Abraham He had to see if Sodom and Gomorrah were as wicked as He had been told. We know that between the two cities there were approximately a quarter of a million people. They were neighboring towns. They were located in what is now the Dead Sea area. They were wicked. We know from what happened later in the chapter that they were very heavily involved in homosexuality. We know from other historical accounts that they were involved in other things that are called an abomination to God.

"And the men turned their faces from thence, and went towards Sodom: but Abraham stood yet before the Lord. And Abraham drew near and said, will you destroy the righteous with the wicked? Peradventure there be fifty righteous within the city: wilt thou also destroy and spare not the place for the fifty righteous that are therein? That be far from thee to do after this manner to slay the righteous with the wicked: and that the righteous should be as the wicked, that be far from thee: Shall not the judge of all earth do right?"

You do not talk to God like that unless you know what you are talking about. Abraham did. Look what he asked Him. You have two towns here, a metroplex of a quarter of a million people — wicked beyond most of our own comprehension. We know from history that they were involved in sacrificing babies to idols. Abraham stands in front of God and intercedes for these cities.

"And the Lord said, If I find in Sodom fifty righteous, within the city, then I will spare all the place for their sakes." For whose sakes? For the sake of the righteous. *"And Abraham answered and said, Behold now, I have taken upon me to speak unto the Lord, which am but dust and ashes: Peradventure there shall lack five of the fifty righteous: wilt thou destroy all the city for lack of five? And he said, If I find there forty and five, I will not destroy it. And he spake unto him yet again, and said, Peradventure there shall be forty found there. And he said I will not do it for forty's sake. And he said unto him, Oh let not the Lord be angry, and I will speak: Peradventure there shall thirty be found there. And he said I will not do it, if I find thirty there. And he said, Behold now I have taken upon me to speak unto the Lord: Peradventure there shall be twenty found there. And he said, I will not destroy it for twenty's*

sake. And he said, Oh let not the Lord be angry, and I will speak yet but this once: Peradventure ten shall be found there. And he said, I will not destroy it for ten's sake." And the Lord went His way and Abraham returned unto his place.

Abraham must have thought, "There is Lot, Lot's wife, two daughters who are not married — that's five. And then the other two daughters who are married, their two husbands and a chance that one of them might have a child. That is ten." But there were not ten. There were only four and one of them did not make it all the way — Lot's wife.

There are several reasons why I wanted us to read this incident. First of all, I want you to see the power of intercession. Abraham stood in the gap for the entire population of Sodom and Gomorrah. Abraham could have brought God all the way down to one. It was not God who was dictating the terms. It was Abraham. He could have brought Him all the way down to one and the cities would have stayed there.

It is important for us to know this because if Abraham could do it, we can do it.

IS JUDGMENT FALLING ON AMERICA?

Lately many preachers are on the same band wagon of declaring that judgment is going to fall on the United States of America. God has more sense than that. If for no other reason, He does not have any other nation on earth that is doing what this country is concerning missions. In addition, the Bible says that where the righteous are exalted the nation is blessed. Yes, there are problems in our nation, but our country is far from going down the drain. Revival is the key to the salvation of the United States of America. This country is not in nearly as bad shape as everybody wants us to think it is. The devil will try to discourage you and get you to give up in your faith and get you to accept problems. Oftentimes he will tell you that the reason why these things are happening is because they are the signs of the times. The reason why these things are happening is because the church is not doing its job of praying, of interceding, or witnessing, of becoming active in the system. Becoming active in the system with prayer and intercession — that is what counts. That is where the power is. It belongs to everyone of us. It is so easy when you know a few things about the Word of God.

Pray and intercede and do combat against the power of darkness. Do not allow bad news to discourage you concerning your country. The Bible says that we are the salt of the earth. As long as we are here this thing is not going to rot. The Bible says the righteous shall never be removed, but the wicked shall be rooted out.

VOICES IN THE LAND

We have a great opportunity. We can stand up in the midst of all this fear and be a voice of exhortation and comfort and voice of victory in the land. You are going to win a lot more people to Jesus Christ doing that than trying to scare them into heaven. We are not here to scare anyone. We are here to get them saved.

Isn't that what we read in Timothy? *"For God desires that all men be saved and come into the knowledge of the truth."* Let us intercede and pray for our country — ask our Father in the name of Jesus to send revival into this land and open the doors of utterance so that we can go forth and minister the Word of God.

"Father, your Word says that you hold the heart of our President in your hand, and you turn it as you will. Turn the heart of our President toward the Word of God. Father, your Word says that you raise up whom you will and you put down whom you will. Remove from positions of authority those who will not listen to your voice. Raise up people who are dedicated, spirit-filled, turned on to the Word of God, to take those positions of authority."

As for me and my house we are going to serve the Lord. As long as we are serving the Lord, He is going to take care of the place where we live. If you are serving the Lord and I am serving the Lord, and if God would have saved Sodom and Gomorrah for ten, don't you believe He will save America with all the Christians we have now? God hates sin but He loves sinners. You have to change men's hearts. The only way you are going to get them to think differently is to get them born again.

Do you know how to get them born again? You create an atmosphere in this nation for revival through intercessory prayer.

PROPER PRIORITIES

We, as churches, must put our priorities straight. We realize that we are the salt of the earth, cities set on a hill that cannot be hid, the light of the world. We must do everything we can to get God's Word out in every form we can and reach people and get them born again. When you get people born again and filled with the Holy Ghost and turned on to the Word of God then you will stop a lot of the filth that is going on in our country today. I know this is a different approach, but it is the only one that will work.

Ezekial 22:30, *"And I sought for a man among them, that should make up the hedge, and stand in the gap before me for the land, that I should not destroy it: but I have found none. Therefore have I poured out mine indignation upon them; I have consumed them with the fire of my wrath; their own way have I recompensed upon their heads, saith the Lord God."* The judgment came, didn't it? But it could have been diverted by how many people? By one man. I am convinced that one church can turn the course of this country.

Intercession is a calling, and you do it. Intercession is when you take hold of something and you pray about it until you see it come into existence. You do not let go. Grab hold of that thing and hold on to it. Pray and stay before God with it. Pray and intercede and fight against the powers of darkness and do spiritual warfare until that thing comes into existence. You need to take time in your prayer time and spend it praying for your nation. You will see inflation curbed and turned back and interest rates come down. You will not have to spend so much time praying about God meeting your needs financially because our economy will settle down.

CHAPTER X
THE PRAYER OF BINDING AND LOOSING

Matthew 18:18, *"Verily I say unto you. Whatsoever ye shall bind on earth shall be bound in heaven: and whatsoever ye shall loose on earth shall be loosed in heaven."* Amplified Bible — *"Truly, I tell you, whatever you forbid and declare to be improper and unlawful on earth must be what is already forbidden in heaven, and whatever you permit and declare proper and lawful on earth must be already permitted in heaven."*

The King James text gives the impression that God is waiting for us to establish the laws that will rule heaven and earth. To a degree this is true. But notice the Amplified translation sheds additional light on this prayer. He said what you forbid and declare to be unlawful on earth must be what is already forbidden in heaven. There are things that go on in the earth that God has already declared to be unlawful. "If God has declared them to be unlawful, then how come they are happening?" Because the authority on this planet was given to men. (Genesis 1:27) God gave us authority on the earth, and our authority is rooted in God. Therefore whatever we forbid and declare to be unlawful must be what is already forbidden in heaven. You cannot stop something from happening on earth that God has not already declared to be unlawful.

I am spending time on this because people read these verses and come up with all kinds of funny ideas. "Satan, I forbid you from doing anything on this planet ever again." That is not forbidden in heaven. He can do things on earth. Adam let him into the planet and he still has the right to be here. But God has declared that you, as one of His children, can stand up and forbid him to manifest himself in your life. You can declare his works in your life unlawful. You can stop what he is doing — you can bind him. God said whatever you permit and declare proper and lawful on earth must already be permitted in heaven.

BINDERS AND LOOSERS

You and I are the binders and loosers. He said you can bind on earth and you can loose on earth. God has already established and it is written down in heaven, the things that He declares to be lawful on the earth, but men must institute that law. This is no different than the nation we live in.

ENFORCING THE LAW

Congress can pass laws until they turn blue in the face, but it will not do any good until the local police officer enforces the law. Do you know that it is not legal in the United States of America for the Mafia to operate? There is not a law in Washington that says the Mafia can operate in the United States of America. We have all kinds of laws forbidding them from doing what they are doing. But do you know when they are going to stop? When the laws are enforced. When people stand up and say, "This is not right, and we are not going to have it any more." Then they will be stopped. But as long as people are willing to tolerate it, then it will keep on happening.

The same thing is true in your life dealing with Satan. God has declared in Colossians 1:13 that Christ has delivered you from the authority of darkness and translated you into the kingdom of His dear Son. You are redeemed (Galatians 3:13) from the curse of the law. You have been set free. Jesus said when you know the truth, the truth will make you free. (John 8:31) Hebrews the second chapter says Jesus came and destroyed the power of the devil. I Peter 2:24 says by His stripes you were healed. Matthew 8:17 says Himself bore your sicknesses and carried your pains. Psalm 103:2-3 says, *"Bless the Lord, O my soul, and forget not all of his benefits: Who forgiveth all thine iniquities; who healeth all thy diseases."* In the mind of God you are already well. He has declared that it is lawful for you to be well. He has declared it. He said that it is lawful for Charles Nieman to be healed. It is lawful for Charles Nieman to be prosperous. It is lawful for Charles Nieman to live in peace. It is lawful for Charles Nieman to be a success. It is lawful for Charles Nieman to get his prayers answered.

There is a network of organized crime working in the spiritual realm on this planet and Satan is the head of it. He is the master thief (John 10:10) and he will take anything away from you that you let him have. "Can we stop him?" You bet we can stop him. You can bind him from your affairs. You can declare and say, "Satan, I forbid you on authority of God's Word." God has given you that authority. If you are waiting for God to do it you are in for a long wait. It is amazing how many times in my own life I will wait around and tolerate things. Do you ever catch yourself tolerating things? While you are in that position the devil will lie to you — he's good at that. He will tell you, "Well, you know that is just the way it is — this is happening in your life because of this and because of that." But after awhile you wake up and you see where you are and where you once were.

LIVING WITH THE CURSE

It is so easy to get busy doing things and after awhile you are living with the curse. I mean just little harrassing things, like a dog nipping at your heels. Not bad enough to bother you, it is just annoying, but you can live with it. And it just goes on and on and it will keep going on until you say "stop it" —until you forbid it.

Let us read it again, *"... Whatever you forbid and declare to be improper and unlawful on earth must be what is already forbidden in heaven ..."* What is forbidden in heaven? I do not have the space to show you all of the things that God has forbidden, from His standpoint, for you.

SHOULD I BIND OR LOOSE?

The King James text says that whatever you bind on earth shall be bound in heaven and whatsoever you loose on earth shall be loosed in heaven. There are some things that need to be loosed and some things that need to be bound. You need to bind the devil and loose the blessings of God. Now, that is not a hard, fast rule. Sometimes you need to loose the devil because he has a grip on someone. Oftentimes the prayer of binding and loosing will move over into intercessory prayer.

A few days ahead of when I do seminars, I bind the demonic forces that would try to stop me from having successful meetings. I bind the spirit of unbelief, the spirit of poverty, the spirit of witchcraft, the spirits of strife, envy and confusion. On the other hand I also loose things I want to have in the meetings. I loose the spirit of healing, the spirit of salvation, the spirit of miracles, etc. — and I tell you, it works.

CHAPTER XI
THE PRAYER OF AGREEMENT

The prayer of agreement is found in Matthew 18:19,20, *"Again I say unto you, That if two of you shall agree on earth as touching anything that they ask, it shall be done for them of my Father which is in heaven. For where two or three are gathered together in my name, there am I in the midst of them."* This is what is commonly called the prayer of agreement.

Deuteronomy 32:30, *"How should one chase a thousand, and two put ten thousand to flight ..."* Matthew 18:19,20 says *"Again I say unto you, That if two* (what can two do? — put ten thousand to flight!) *of you shall agree on earth as touching anything that they shall ask, it shall be done for them of my Father which is in heaven. For where two or three are gathered together in my name, there am I in the midst of them."* Why is Jesus in the midst of them that have gathered in His name? He is there to make sure that the thing that they agreed on is carried out! He is there to enforce your agreement, to make sure that the agreement comes to pass the exact way you prayed.

Now this is a very powerful type of prayer. A lot of people use this type of prayer. I have people constantly come to me and say, "Will you agree with me concerning this situation?" This is one of the most tremendous, dynamic type of prayers that God has given us.

THE PROPER FOUNDATION

But there is some basic ground work that must be laid to see it function properly. First of all, the two people who are going to do the praying must be in agreement. It is foolish for people to pray and agree together concerning a situation if they are not in agreement. There is no way they can pray the prayer of agreement and have it work.

Amplified Bible, verse 19, *"Again I tell you if two of you on earth agree, harmonize together, make a symphony about anything and everything, whatever they shall ask, it will come to pass and be done for them by my Father in heaven."* What did He say you had to do? The foundation for the prayer of agreement is agreement or harmony.

Now, that harmony must be in several areas. The first area is very obvious. You must agree about the very need you are praying about. For example, you may come to me and say, "Charles, I want you to agree with me that God will give me five thousand dollars." It is possible that at that given moment my faith is not working at a five thousand dollar level. I may be handling all I can handle with my faith. I have told people before when they asked me to agree with them that I could not at that time. Sometimes they looked at me so discouragingly. I am going to be honest with people. I am not going to agree with them in prayer if I know I cannot stand in faith with them. I would rather a person be discouraged with me than disappointed with God because their prayer was not answered.

The prayer of agreement will not work if one of the people is in faith and the other one is in fear. You need to be careful whom you ask to agree with you.

One of the most powerful forms of agreement in the earth is when a husband and wife pray together and agree as touching something. That is why Satan is trying so hard to break up marriages.

You will not see the prayer of agreement work as well as it can unless the people who are praying live free from strife. A person cannot walk around in strife and contention all the time and then expect to be able to pray the prayer of agreement whenever they choose. To pray the prayer of agreement, you need to live a life of agreement. You need to live in agreement all the time. You cannot be in strife with one person and attempt to pray the prayer of agreement with another person. Mark 11:25 shows us that prayer will not work in a person's life who is in strife. *"And when you stand praying, forgive..."*

CHAPTER XII
THE PRAYER OF DEDICATION

Luke 22:39, "And he came out, and went, as he was wont, to the mount of Olives; and his disciples also followed him. And when he was at the place, he said unto them, Pray that ye enter not into temptation. And he was withdrawn from them about a stone's cast, and kneeled down and prayed."

Jesus is in the garden of Gethsemane. It is right after the last supper. The disciples have come with Him. He has left them and walked away to pray. Listen to what He prays — *"...Father, if thou be willing, remove this cup from me: nevertheless not my will, but thine, be done. And there appeared an angel unto him from heaven, strengthening him. And being in an agony he prayed more earnestly: and his sweat was as it were great drops of blood falling down to the ground."*

The book of Hebrews tells us that Jesus resisted temptation to the point of blood. There is a condition which can occur in a person's body when he comes under intense pressure. He becomes so emotionally enthralled in something, that his capillaries, which lie directly underneath the skin, begin to burst. Blood will actually ooze from the pores. That is what happened to Jesus. The cross put that much pressure on Him. He knew the horror that awaited Him there — the pain, the anguish, the hurt, the shame. When He would finally be relieved of that physical pain, then the greatest torment was yet to come. He had to go to hell — a place of torture, pain and suffering. In the face of that, look at what Jesus prayed. People think that Jesus was superhuman and that He did not have a desire to live. If anyone had a desire to live, it was Jesus. He knew how to live. He was in the prime of His life — thirty-three years old. He knelt down and said, *"Father, if you are willing, remove this cup from me. Nevertheless, not my will but your will be done."* Jesus dedicated Himself to the will of God.

"IF"

This is the only type of prayer that Jesus ever prayed and that you can pray where you can insert the word "if" and be scriptural. This is a one-time prayer, when you seriously and purposely commit your life to do God's will. The prayer of dedication sounds something like this, "Father, I will to do Your will whatever it is. If You want me to go here, I will go. If You want me to do this, I will do it. If You want me not to do that, I will not do it. I will to do Your will whatever it might be. Not my will but Your will."

The prayer of dedication is when you dedicate yourself to the will of God. This type of prayer is never used in the realm of petitioning. If you pray, "Father, I am asking You to give me this if it be Your will," do not even bother to pray. If you do not know it is the will of God for you to have something or not before you pray, then do not even bother to pray. I John 5 says that God hears prayers that are prayed according to His will. If you do not know God's will, putting that little tag on your prayer is not going to guarantee that He is going to hear it. Also, do not use the prayer of dedication when you are asking for forgiveness. For example, "Father, in the name of Jesus, I am never going to do that again. I am never going to do that again. From this day forward it is your will for me and that is all." People think God will forgive them because they pray that way. No. That is not the prayer of forgiveness. The prayer of forgiveness is, "Father, I did wrong and I confess it to you. I am asking you to forgive me in the name of Jesus."

I John 1:9 says God is faithful and just to forgive us of our sins when we confess them to Him, and to cleanse us from all unrighteousness. Once you pray and ask God to forgive you, then if you want to pray the prayer of dedication that is fine. But do not try to use the prayer of dedication to receive forgiveness. You need to pray and dedicate yourself to the will of God. You may have to pray it more than once. If you get out of the will of God for a time you might want to recommit yourself to God's will — that is fine.

Did you see what happened to Jesus when He prayed that prayer? Luke 22:43, *"And there appeared an angel unto Him from heaven, strengthening Him."* God sent a messenger, an angel, to come and help Him and strengthen Him as only an angel can do. Sometimes it is not easy to do the will of God. Sometimes it is just easier to flow with the crowd. Sometimes you need extra strength. God will help you. God will help you stand up in the face of adversity and ridicule.

The prayer of dedication is a prayer that only you can pray for yourself. I cannot pray it for you. You must pray it for yourself. You need to pray the prayer of dedication sometime in your life. I wrote my prayer of dedication down on paper. Every once in a while I get it out and reread it just to remind myself of what I told God. God is not the one who forgets. Do not make promises to God that you do not intend to keep, because God does not forget, and He will not let you forget.

CHAPTER XIII
PRAYER OF COMMITTAL

Luke 18:1, *"And he spake a parable unto them to this end, that we ought always to pray and not to faint."* Now one translation says that men ought always to pray and not give up or not cave in. You can have a prayer life which is ineffective. If you are praying and nothing is happening then you are not praying correctly, and you are not praying effectively, you are not praying scripturally.

God did not design prayer to be a means whereby you tell God your problems. Matthew 6:32 says that God knows what you have need of even before you ask Him. God is well aware of every situation in your life. God is well aware of what is going on in our lives. He is very conscious of where we are and what we are doing.

What then is the purpose for prayer? Is prayer just something that we do? Is it just a part of being a good Christian? Are we supposed to pray and keep God happy? Is prayer just something that we do?

Prayer is God's invitation to us to come and fellowship with Him. Prayer is God's invitation to you to come and fellowship with Him.

CARE-FREE, NOT CARE-LESS

Philippians 4:6, *"Be careful for nothing; but in every thing by prayer and supplication with thanksgiving let your requests be made known unto God.-"* God said "be careful for nothing." Now, He did not say "do nothing." He said do not be careful or worrisome or anxious or fretful. The word "careful" in verse 6 comes from the same Greek word that is found in Mark 4 where Jesus said that the cares of this world, entering in, would choke the Word of God and make it become unfruitful. It is the Greek word "merimna" which literally translated means anxiety, fretfulness, care, concern, solicitude — better known as worry.

I have discovered when some people say, "That is not my care" their meaning of that statement and my understanding of that statement are two different things. What they are saying is that they are not going to think about it, they are not going to do anything about it, they are not going to make any effort to get it worked out, they are just going to play like it is not there. In other words, they are going to stick their heads up in the clouds and not think about the situation. There is a difference between being careful about something and doing what needs to be done spiritually.

Now, I do not worry — I refuse to worry or fret about anything, including my church. I am not going to worry about my church, but that does not mean that I do not have responsibilities concerning it. I pray for it. I intercede on behalf of it. I do my homework before I teach. I make sure that I can hear the spirit of God. I stay sensitive to Him.

We still have responsibilities even though we are carefree. He says, *"Be careful for nothing, but in everything by prayer and supplication with thanksgiving let your requests be made known unto God. And the peace of God which passeth all understanding, shall keep your hearts and minds through Christ Jesus."* He said for us not to worry about the situation — pray about it! Let your requests be made known unto God. Do not just ignore the thing and treat it like it does not exist because it will not go away. The problem will stay until you do something about it in your prayer life. It will stay until you bring that request before God.

THANKSGIVING AND FAITH

Thanksgiving is the end result of faith. What would you think if I walked up to you and said, "Thank you." You would probably say, "For what?" The only reason I would say "thank you" is because you have done something for me or you have given me something.

Thanksgiving is the response that comes from somebody else's action towards you, and it is an action that you like. The same thing is true here. Now remember, the foundation of prayer is faith. Jesus said in the book of Matthew, *"...whatsoever ye shall ask in prayer, believing ye shall receive."* He said in Mark 11:24, *"Therefore I say unto you, what things soever ye desire, when ye pray, believe you receive them, and ye shall have them."* If I am confident of God's will to answer my prayer, I therefore believe I receive when I pray. The natural thing then is for me to give God thanks. Thanksgiving will flow from me. My mother raised me to say "thank you" when someone did something for me as a favor. The same thing is true when it comes to praying and receiving from God.

Thanksgiving is the natural fruit of a healthy prayer life — a prayer life that is based on faith in God's Word, faith in God's promises, faith in God's love. When you are convinced of God's love for you when you pray, and you know that God hears you, and you have His promise that whatsoever things you ask Him in prayer believing you shall receive them — thanksgiving will follow.

THE CLOAK OF HUMILITY

I Peter 5:5, *"Likewise, ye younger, submit yourselves unto the elder. Yea, all of you be subject one to another, and be clothed with humility: for God resisteth the proud, and giveth grace to the humble."* I think verse five is one of the most outstanding verses of scripture concerning the body of Christ that exists.

Look again at what he said, *"Likewise, ye younger, submit yourselves unto the elder. Yea, all of you be subject ..."* How many of us? All of us. Who is he talking to — he is talking to everyone of us isn't he? He said, *"Likewise, ye younger, submit yourselves unto the elder. Yea, all of you be subject one to another ..."* Be subject one to another. I am subject to you and you are subject to me. Are we subject to each other to where we have the right to tell each other what to do in every area of our lives? By no means. I do not want the responsibility for making all the decisions in your life. I have enough decisions in my own life to make. He said be subject one to another.

The word "subject" carries a special meaning with it of being sensitive to the needs of one another, being aware of one another, being available to help one another, being available to take the needs of somebody else and make them first place in your life, along with yours or being willing to be a servant in the body of Christ.

"Likewise, ye younger, submit yourselves unto the elder. Yea, all of you be subject one to another, and be clothed with humility ..." In the Greek text the word "clothed" has a meaning of putting on a cloak of humility. When we come together I am supposed to see humility on you and you are supposed to see humility on me. We are all supposed to be clothed with humility.

THE IMMOVABLE WALL

"...For God resisteth the proud, but giveth grace unto the humble." If you want to know what it is like to push against an immovable wall then get God to resist you. Would you like to fight through God to obtain something? Hopeless would be a good word for that. He said that God would resist the proud, but He will give grace to the humble. If I want God to give me grace, and not resist me, then I am going to have to become a humble man.

Do you want God's grace? Then you must be humble.

BIBLE HUMILITY

What is humility then? He tells us in I Peter 5:6,7, *"Humble yourselves therefore under the mighty hand of God, that he may exalt you in due time: Casting all your care upon him; for he careth for you."*

"I'm no good. I'm just a worm. I'm good for nothing. I don't deserve anything from God." Is that Bible humility? No, no, a thousand times no! The whole point of redemption is that God did not leave you a "no-good-for-nothing." He did not commend His love towards you and make you a "new no-good-for-nothing." If that were the case, He would have left you the way you were. That was the reason Jesus told Nicodemus that he must be born again. You stopped being a "no-good-for-nothing" when you became a child of the most high God. You also became the righteousness of God in Christ (II Corinthians 5:21) and an heir of God and a joint heir with Jesus Christ. (Romans 8:14,16)

Sure, you may have problems and there may be some things in you that need to be straightened out, but God sees you conformed to the image of His dear Son. (Romans 8:29) As far as He is concerned, you are going to make it. God sees you as a winner! Revelation 1:6 says that you are a king and a priest in the household of God.

HUMBLE YOURSELF

Notice God does not humble anyone. He said for you to humble yourself. God does not want puppets. God does not want you to do anything because He grabs you by the neck and sticks your face in the dirt and says, "Now you will worship me or I will smash you like a bug." God will bring you to Him by His love and then you will give Him your worship because you want to, not because you have to. God is not going to humble you. He said for you to humble yourself under the mighty hand of God. Do you know what is going to happen to you? *"Humble yourselves therefore under the mighty hand of God, that he may exalt you in due time."* God will exalt you. God is not against man being exalted. He is against their exalting themselves because they get puffed up and cannot see clearly since their heads are swollen out of proportion.

"Humble yourselves therefore under the mighty hand of God, that he may exalt you in due time." God wants to exalt you. Do you desire for your children to live better than you? God wants to lift you up out of the miry clay and put you on the rock to stay.

How do you humble yourself under the mighty hand of God? By, *"Casting all your care upon him; for he careth for you."* There are two Greek words used for "care" in this verse. The first one means anxiety, worry, fretfulness. He said cast all your anxiety, your worry and your fretfulness upon God because He cares for you. The second one means that He loves you affectionately. God loves you and wants you to take the care, the things that worry you, that cause anxiety in your life and roll them over on Him. When you pray that prayer you are saying, "I am taking my life and I am putting it in your hands. I am taking this situation and I am putting it in your hands." By doing that you are humbling yourself under the mighty hand of God. You are recognizing that He is more powerful than you, that He has greater abilities than you do. You are saying to Him and to all the world that you are taking God's power and His will for your life.

Worry will nullify your prayer faster than anything else. Worry does not change anything except you. It will change the way your body functions. Worry will change your attitude. He said humble yourself therefore under the mighty hand of God. Many people need to pray this prayer for their husbands, wives and children. Sure they have responsibilities to take care of them. They need to pray for them, but they do not need to worry about them.

In verse eight he continues talking to us about what we should do after we have cast our cares over on the Lord. *"Be sober, be vigilant; because your adversary the devil, as a roaring lion, walketh about, seeking whom he may devour: Whom resist steadfast in the faith, knowing that the same afflictions are accomplished in your brethren that are in the world."* What are you supposed to do about the devil? Resist him. How? Steadfast in the faith. That means unwavering, sure, steady.

YOU'RE NOT THE ONLY ONE

It was quite a revelation to me when I discovered that I was not the only one whom the devil was after.

It helped me to resist and defeat him as I watched and learned from other people. All of us must overcome problems. There are some people who think they are under some kind of heavy load, and they might be. I know a lot of people who are going through things that make other people's problems look like a church picnic.

We need to keep problems in the right perspective and not allow them to be blown out of proportion to the extent that we think nobody has it as badly as we do. He said all of these afflictions are accomplished in our brethren who are in the world.

Satan will labor to make the problem get bigger in your sight and eventually it becomes so big that you cannot handle it anymore and it seems there is no remedy available. But there is a remedy in God's Word.

By praying God's Word and by being strong in faith you can overcome any circumstance. Remember, you are more than conquerors through Christ Jesus who loves you! (Romans 8:37)

CHAPTER XIV
UNITED PRAYER

Acts 3, Peter and John were on their way to the temple several days after the day of Pentecost when they came upon a man who sat by the gate Beautiful who was a cripple. Something was wrong with the bones in his ankles. He could not walk. Peter and John fastened their eyes on him and Peter said for him to look on them. The man looked up expecting to receive alms and Peter said that he did not have any money to give him to make his life better, but what he did have to make him better, he would give it to him. He then said, *"...In the name of Jesus Christ of Nazareth rise up and walk."* And he reached down and took the man by his hand and pulled him up to his feet and immediately his ankle bones were made strong and the man ran, leaping and praising and glorifying God through the temple. The religious leaders did not like that so they took Peter and John before the high priest. He was the same man who just a few days before had crucified the Lord Jesus Christ.

Acts 4:4, *"Howbeit many of them which heard the word believed; and the number of the men was about five thousand. And it came to pass on the morrow, that their rulers, and elders, and scribes, And Annas the high priest, and Caiaphas, and John, and Alexander, and as many as were of the kindred of the high priest, were gathered together at Jerusalem. And when they had set them in the midst, they asked, By what power, or by what name, have ye done this? Then Peter, filled with the Holy Ghost, said unto them, Ye rulers of the people, and elders of Israel, If we this day examined of the good deed done to the impotent man, by what means he is made whole; Be it known unto you all, and to all the people of Israel, that by the name of Jesus Christ of Nazareth, whom ye crucified, whom God raised from the dead, even by him doth this man stand here before you whole. This is the stone which was set at nought of you builders, which is become the head of the corner. Neither is there salvation in any other: for there is none other name under heaven given among men, whereby we must be saved. Now when they saw the boldness of Peter and John, and perceived that they were unlearned and ignorant men, they marvelled; and they took knowledge of them, that they had been with Jesus. And beholding the man which was healed standing with them, they could say nothing against it. But when they had commanded them to go aside out of the council, they conferred among themselves, Saying, What shall we do to these men? for that indeed a notable miracle hath been done by them is manifest to all them that dwell in Jerusalem; and we cannot deny it. That it spread no further among the people, let us straitly threaten them, that they speak henceforth to no man in this name. And they called them, and commanded them not to speak at all nor teach in the name of Jesus. But Peter and John answered and said unto them, whether it be right in the sight of God to hearken unto you more than unto God, judge ye. For we cannot but speak the things which we have seen and heard. So when they had further threatened them, they let them go, finding nothing how they might punish them, because of the people: for all men glorified God for that which was done."*

Now go on to verse 23, *"And being let go, they went to their own company, and reported all that the chief priests and elders had said unto them. And when they heard that, they lifted up their voice to God with one accord, and said, Lord, thou art God, which hast made heaven and earth, and the sea, and all that in them is: Who by the mouth of thy servant David hast said, Why did the heathen rage, and the people imagine vain things? The kings of the earth stood up, and the rulers were gathered together against the Lord, and against his Christ. For of a truth against thy holy child Jesus, whom thou hast anointed, both Herod, and Pontius Pilate, with the Gentiles, and the people of Israel, were gathered together. For to do whatsoever thy hand and thy counsel determined before to be done. And now, Lord, behold their threatenings: and grant unto thy servants, that with all boldness they may speak thy word, By stretching forth thine hand to heal; and that signs and wonders may be done by the name of the holy child Jesus. And when they had prayed, the place was shaken where they were assembled together; and they were all filled with the Holy Ghost, and they spake the word of God with boldness."*

This is an excellent example of what is called united prayer. Peter and John came back from the presence of the elders. They came into their own company. By that time we know that the church of Jerusalem was already around 9,000 or 10,000 people. Three thousand were saved on the day of Pentecost and 5,000 were saved the day that the lame man was healed. That is 8,000, not counting how many more had been coming in day by day. So they went back and reported to all of the people what had been said to them and they prayed. Notice, they lifted up their voices with one accord. It is commonly believed that the disciples and the people who were with them formed a prayer and then everybody prayed it together.

If you will look carefully, you will discover that the prayer they prayed came directly from the Old Testament. I like the way they prayed, don't you? *"...Lord, behold their threatenings: and grant unto thy servants that with all boldness they may speak thy word."* Notice, they did not say, "Father, we are asking you to somehow work out a compromise between us and them." These men purposed within themselves to go on teaching the Word. They said, *"...grant unto thy servants that with all boldness they may speak thy word."* It was the speaking of the Word that they had been threatened not to do anymore.

They prayed a united prayer. There is great power in united prayer. Oftentimes we will see a need arise which will affect all of us. You may be facing problems that I am not facing. I might not be affected by them. On the other hand, there may be things that come up in our nation or against the church that affect all of us. In that case, we need to do as they did and unite ourselves together, form a prayer, and then all of us pray it together, and watch God move! In the fifth chapter, the fifteenth verse, we see how the Lord responded to the prayer. *"Insomuch that they brought forth the sick into the streets, and laid them on beds and couches, that at the least the shadow of Peter passing by might overshadow some of them. There came also a multitude out of the cities round about unto Jerusalem bringing sick folks, and them which were vexed with unclean spirits: and they were healed every one."*

CHAPTER XV
PRAYING FOR YOUR FOOD

I Timothy 4:1, *"Now the Spirit speaketh expressly, that in the latter times some shall depart from the faith, giving heed to seducing spirits, and doctrines of devils."* Now, what does he mean by a seducing spirit? In these latter days, Satan will release against you and me demonic spirits that will try to lure us away from the things of God, away from the faith that was delivered to us. The Word says that some will fall away from the faith because they heed to these seducing spirits. What is a devil's doctrine? Well, let's read some of them — he lists some here. *"Speaking lies in hypocrisy..."* The word "lies" is an interesting word in the Greek text. Hebrews 4:12 says, *"For the Word of God is quick, and powerful, and sharper than any two-edged sword, piercing even to the dividing asunder of soul and spirit, and of the joints and marrow, and is a discerner of the thoughts and intents of the heart."* In the Greek text the word "Word" in Hebrews 4:12 is the Greek word logos. There are two different words used in the Greek text for the Word of God —there is "logos" and there is "rhema". Rhema refers to the spoken word. Logos refers to the entire Word of God, primarily, that which is revealed and that which is written. Rhema talks about the spoken word — the word that is spoken out of your mouth. Romans 10:17 says, *"So then faith cometh by hearing, and hearing by the word of God."* (Rhema) In the Greek text, "lies" is the Greek word psuedologos. That means it sounds like the Word, it looks like the Word, but it is not the Word.

You must be careful what you listen to. There are a lot of teachings floating around today being called "Christian material". Some of it is outstanding and some of it is garbage. There are some who desire to tell us things that sound like the Word of God and they know what they are saying is wrong, but they are trying to lure us into their camp. We must *"...Take heed what ye hear."* (Mark 4:24) *"Forbidding to marry, and commanding to abstain from meats,* (two more doctrines of devils) *which God hath created to be received with thanksgiving of them which believe and know the truth. For every creature of God is good, and nothing to be refused, if it be received with thanksgiving: For it is sanctified by the word of God and prayer."*

The Word of God will sanctify the food that you put in your mouth. I am convinced that a part of the curse would be to live in El Paso and not be able to eat Mexican food. That would be terrible. He said, if we will do what He said to do, what we eat will not hurt us. He said, if we receive our food with thanksgiving, it is sanctified by the Word of God and prayer. What is the Word of God that sanctifies your food? In Mark 16, Jesus said that believers shall go forth and if they eat any deadly thing it shall not hurt them. I have gone into restaurants before with people and prayed over my food in faith. I was the only one who did not get sick later. You had better pray when you eat in restaurants. I worked in a fancy restaurant when I was in college. I know what goes on in those kitchens. You had better pray over your food, and don't be embarrassed when you pray!

EXAMPLE OF SMITH WIGGLESWORTH

I am not advocating that you be like Smith Wigglesworth. He was in a cafeteria one time in London. A young man was with him and Smith said for him to pray over the food. So the man prayed one of those, "I'm not really praying. I'm rubbing my head because I have a headache prayer." He looked up and Smith was looking at him and he said, "I said, pray over the food." The man prayed the same way again. When he got through, he looked up and Smith was leaning across the table at him and said, "Pray over the food." The young man looked around the room, and bowing his head, prayed again. This time when he looked up, Smith was standing up looking at him. He said, "I will do it" and Smith threw his hands up and his voice boomed across the restaurant and the whole place stopped. Smith proceeded to pray for the food and the sinners who were in there that God would convict their dark hearts. When he got through, he sat down and started eating, but the rest of the people were in shock.

When they left, the young man asked Smith, "Why did you pray like that?" He said, "I had their attention, I might as well use it." If you care what that food is going to do when it gets inside you, you better pray for it while it is still on the plate. He said, *"For every creature of God is good, and nothing to be refused, if it be received with thanksgiving: For it is sanctified by the Word of God in prayer."*

Yes, I believe that you should watch what you eat, but do not put your trust in eating right to keep you well. Proverbs 4:22 tells us that the Word is medicine to our flesh.

CHAPTER XVI
A CHECK LIST FOR EFFECTIVE PRAYERS

Number one — The physical position that you are in when you pray is of no importance at all. Jesus prayed looking up to heaven, with his eyes open, with his eyes closed, looking down, walking, standing, sitting and lying down. The physical position does affect your attitude. There is something about getting down on my knees and praying that makes me get serious, but you do not have to be on your knees to pray. The physical position is not important.

Number two — Always remember to pray to the Father in the name of Jesus.

Number three — Believe that you receive when you pray. Now that is not something that just happens. It is the result of knowing God's Word when you pray, knowing God's will concerning your prayer and bringing them together in prayer. The fundamental rock upon which prayer is built is trust. You trust God to keep His Word. If you do not have that foundation in your prayer life, you are not going to have an effective prayer life.

Number four — According to Mark 11:25-26 forgive when you pray. If you have strife in your heart when you pray, your prayer will not produce. Jesus said that if we do not forgive them who trespass against us our heavenly Father will not forgive us our trespasses. Unforgiveness will shut down your prayer life. I think of all the things that Jesus told us to do, forgiveness is one of the hardest. The Bible says that we can, and we are to forgive, even as God forgives. How does God forgive? He forgives and forgets.

Number five — Remember to depend on the Holy

Spirit in your prayer life. Allow him to help and aid you. Pray the prayer of intercession and pray for other people. Spend time edifying yourself by praying in other tongues. Jude 20, *"But ye beloved, building up yourselves on your most holy faith, praying in the Holy Ghost, keep yourselves in the love of God, looking for the mercy of our Lord Jesus Christ unto eternal life."*

He said for us to build ourselves up praying in the Holy Ghost. The word "build" means "charge up". You charge yourself up when you pray in the spirit. You may not feel charged up, but you will get that way if you spend time praying in the Spirit.

Praying in the spirit also keeps you in the love of God. Strife has never done one good thing for anybody who has ever lived. The book of James says where you find envy and strife you will find confusion and every evil work. When I get confused and I do not know what God wants me to do, I check my "Forgiver". If it is plugged up, I clean it out by asking God to forgive me for being unforgiving, then I pray and forgive the person who hurt me. Once you get into the habit of forgiving, you will find it easier to forgive than to get into strife.